Reclaiming
the
Principalship

TOM MARSHALL

Reclaiming the Principalship

**Instructional Leadership Strategies to Engage
Your School Community and Focus on Learning**

Foreword by
Christopher Lehman

HEINEMANN
Portsmouth, NH

Heinemann

361 Hanover Street

Portsmouth, NH 03801–3912

www.heinemann.com

Offices and agents throughout the world

"Dedicated to Teachers" is a trademark of Greenwood Publishing Group, Inc.

Cataloging-in-Publication Data is on file with the Library of Congress.

ISBN 978-0-325-09251-5

Editor: Tobey Antao

Production Editor: Sonja S. Chapman

Typesetter: Gina Poirier Design

Cover and interior designs: Monica Ann Crigler

Manufacturing: Steve Bernier

Printed in the United States of America on acid-free paper

22   21   20   19   18   PAH   1   2   3   4   5

To Kende, Timi, and Hanga, who bring such joy to all they learn, and to my Marta who keeps me learning through our joy

Contents

Foreword by Christopher Lehman *ix*

Acknowledgments *xii*

Introduction Reclaim the Principalship *xiv*

Chapter 1 Get Smarter with a Professional Network *1*

Build a professional network with other principals to share knowledge and support

Chapter 2 Coach Teachers to Improve Student Learning *27*

Coach teachers sustainably, with a plan to improve instruction across the school

Chapter 3 Manage Your School with Learning in Mind *51*

Put learning before management in leadership decisions by researching issues and working collaboratively

Chapter 4 Evaluate to Support Teachers' and Students' Learning *83*

Evaluate teachers honestly, constructively, and supportively to encourage both teacher engagement and student learning

Chapter 5 Unite and Lead the School Community with Learning Themes *112*

Lead the school community with a unified vision of your school community's goals

Chapter 6 Nurture the Learner Within *133*

Strengthen yourself by honoring your own personal learning

References *149*

HOW TO ACCESS ONLINE RESOURCES

The reproducible tools in this book are also available to download and print:

1. Go to www.heinemann.com.

2. Click on the link in the upper right to **Log In**. *If you do not already have an account with Heinemann, you will need to create an account.*

3. Register your product by entering the code: **RECPRIN**

4. Once you have registered your product, it will appear in the list of **My Online Resources.**

Foreword

Foreword

F amilies drop their children off at school each day on the promise and prayer that we will make their children's lives greater than their own. Every parent, every guardian wants this. As the hands separate and car doors, bus doors, or school doors close, we are given each family's absolute, greatest gift. We are entrusted with this mighty wish. We become a vessel of hope.

The most talented leaders I know are driven to cultivate this hope and promise across their school community. This work is not simple. It means keeping the transactional duties that grow like invasive weeds at bay. It means focusing the greatest time, patience and fertile soil on growing every classroom, every staff member, every leader, into the greatest versions of themselves.

Ancient forests of Douglas Firs and Redwoods have thrived for hundreds, often thousands, of years because well below the surface, deep within the earth, they form a connected community of nutrient sharing. Emerging research is revealing vast networks of overlapping root systems, fungi, and organic materials that funnel nourishment from tree to tree. When we stand at one of these massive trunks and gaze up at their tremendous height, it is the rich life beneath our feet that allow them to flourish. As the poet, Aimee Nezhukumatathil writes: "The secret of soil is that it is alive."

Who benefits most from these connections below-the-surface? The saplings.

Growing just inches above the forest floor, largely in shadow, the youngest of these ancient conifers are at the greatest risk of not surviving. So, below the earth, ancient trees hold one another's outstretched hands. It appears trees connect to one another so they can funnel the greatest percentage of nutrients to their saplings. Across their organic, underground networks, life-sustaining food is passed between adults and out to children. Together, they advance the next generation.

When my friend Tom Marshall first invited me to visit his school in Paramus, NJ, he did so with pride. I think he literally used the words: "I am so proud." I stopped by after a day with a nearby district and together we walked the halls. As educators do, teachers were still in the building well into the afternoon: planning together, tutoring students, or setting up for the next day. Every room we walked into—every room—Tom gushed:

> *"Can you show Chris the supply room you advocated for? Chris, this is amazing!"*

> *"Tell Chris about what you're working on in writing. Chris, you won't believe this."*

> *"Chris, this teacher has created a system the rest of the staff can't stop talking about."*

In turn, teachers talked about their students, their work, and their colleagues with the same awe. I heard in their voices echoes of Tom's energy. Or maybe, it was in his I heard echoes of theirs:

> *"I am so proud of this student, you won't believe what a breakthrough he's made!"*

> *"My colleague is so brilliant, she came up with this idea and I borrowed it."*

> *"Tom asked this amazing question and we just took off."*

Tom Marshall is one of those leaders who understands that the full promise of a school building, a school district, and of our profession, is only realized through building deep and lasting connections, well below the surface. Connections that nourish every member of the community.

His ability to create and nurture these networks of possibility is breathtaking. While always purposeful and mission-driven, they appear to grow as organically as a tree line creeps up a mountain side. He has helped develop a thriving school and district community; an ever-growing series of annual Paramus Summer Literacy Institutes that draw speakers and participants from across the country; a network of school leaders focused on improving literacy called the New Jersey Literacy Leaders' Network. Each is fueled by and filled with the hopes, concerns, learning and beliefs of their members' communities.

Now, through this gift of *Reclaiming the Principalship*, Tom is helping us all build these rich connections across our own communities, ones that can thrive below-the-surface and raise ourselves and our children higher.

Tom writes as he leads, with a full heart, clarity of purpose, and a humble brilliance. As chapters unfold it is clear how tendrils have grown to and through the work in these pages. It is a book grounded in his own deep knowledge of literacy and literacy leadership, polished by long-standing networks of learning with others, and—as Tom always does—one that celebrates, with his infectious joy and wonder, the voices of adults and children.

This is a book I want in every leader's hands. I want it in your hands because yours is a too often solitary, too often weight-of-the-world-heavy role. I want it in your hands because, somehow, despite the struggles and frustrations, you fight every day to get us all to the hope and promise of education. The practices described in *Reclaiming the Principalship* will give energy, hope, and deeper literacy learning to you and your community because they will be made of your community.

Ecology Researcher Dr. Suzanne Simard says of ancient trees' self-organizing networks: "it's those relationships that really build the forest." When a child leaves their family each day and walks through our doors it is our connections to one another—the ways we learn together, think together, grow together—that nurture us so we may see our children, all children, thrive beyond our wildest dreams.

—Christopher Lehman

Acknowledgments

I didn't write this book alone. I share its authorship with many others.

I share it with the teachers of Stony Lane Elementary School, who have helped me write the story of what it means to work with a small group of dedicated professionals who go out of their way to serve children and learn from one another. There is no other school like ours! I am so proud to work with each of you!

I share it with my colleagues in the New Jersey Literacy Leaders' Network, the Paramus Coaching Course, and the Littogether Think Tank and Teacher Leader Project, who remind me each day that teaching and learning are just much, much richer when you're together and not isolated, as it is so easy to become.

I share it with Lucy Calkins and my former colleagues at the Teachers College Reading & Writing Project, who showed me the power of the net-work…of smart people working together with the knowledge that all of us are smarter than any of us.

I share it with my friends in the Hungarian Scout Association, who gave me, as they did with many young people, a first taste of leadership and of working with children. They taught me that humble leadership builds communities of good work, the best in fact!

I share it with Ralph Gioseffi, Elizabeth Spurlock, Danielle DaGiau, Barbara Freeman, and the many other principals I watched before I myself occupied the principal's office, who put learning first in the decisions they made. I share it with Dr. James Montesano and Dr. Joseph Lupo, who gave me my first chance at being the head learner of my own school in Paramus.

I share it with my friends Katherine Bomer, Sandra Wilde, Kathy Doyle, Kathy Collins, Chris Lehman, and many others who encouraged me to tell this story of instructional leadership in the form of this book, so that I could learn more about it through this larger audience.

I share it with Tobey Antao, my editor at Heinemann. I used to read the acknowledgments in the beginning of books where people called their editors giving, patient, and true partners in the journey of writing a book. I did not really understand this until I worked with Tobey.

I share it with Vicki Boyd, Sonja Chapman, Patty Adams, Amanda Bondi, Sarah Fournier, Lisa Fowler, Elizabeth Silvis, and Brett Whitmarsh at Heinemann, for making this book a possibility.

I share it with two families: the one I came from with my parents and brother, who taught me the value of learning, and the one I have made with my lovely wife Marta and amazing children Kende, Timi, and Hanga who keep me learning with wonder throughout my life.

I share it with you for taking the time to read this book and somehow take what's written in it and make it your own to create better worlds for kids and for teachers in learning leadership. Had I not believed you could do it, I wouldn't have taken the time to write it.

Thank you co-authors! Now let's go do some great work!

Introduction
Introduction

RECLAIM THE PRINCIPALSHIP

The principal is pulled in too many directions . . . essentially, initiative overload. It's hard to become an expert in anything and raise the capacity of your staff in those things if you are asked to become "good enough" at dozens of things requiring your attention.

Keeping teachers' morale and confidence positive as they deal with the pressures of new legislation, while attempting to take risks with teaching practices and implementing new programs with the fear of "doing it wrong [is probably my biggest challenge as a leader]."

I have many more students with ODD [oppositional defiant disorder], OCD [obsessive-compulsive disorder], ADD/ADHD [attention-deficit/hyperactivity disorder], and with anxiety than ever before. The issue is that I just do not have the staff to support these growing needs, which falls on me more and more. There are days that are solely devoted to meeting with students, making them feel safe and nurtured, and not addressing any academics all day. It is tough.

My principal when I was a VP [vice-principal] used to have a joke about time management. We were in a K–8 school that was really a management nightmare. He'd say at the end of the day, "So, what did you do to be an instructional leader today?" It was a joke because we were totally stuck on putting out fires and addressing urgent but not-so-important issues all day every day, for the most part.

The comments above are from real principals in real schools.

The early twenty-first century is not an easy time to be a school leader. Changes have swept the educational landscape. The standards movement has evolved into rigorous learning benchmarks that principals must now know quite well to support teachers in their implementation. Changes to teacher and principal evaluation have added new layers of (questionable) accountability for teachers and principals. In some states, 30 percent of a principal's evaluation depends on standardized test results, often with expectations that might sometimes exceed student ability, and further complicated by the fact that these principals don't directly teach the students taking the tests. In the age of cutbacks in the name of financial responsibility, support teacher and instructional aide positions are cut, further obstructing student success. Fewer schools have assistant principals to share the administrative load, making the principal's work even more isolating.

It is, as one of the principals quoted above said, "tough."

Someone once told me that whenever you gain something new in life, you lose something. When we grow up, we gain the independence of adulthood, but we lose the innocence of childhood. We gain responsibility, but lose the safety nets we may have had as children. When we get married, we gain a new type of family, but we lose the independence of the single life. When our children are born, we gain new little people who want to love us more than anything, but we lose the ability to pick up and go whenever we'd like to on a moment's notice.

This is true also when we take on leadership in education. We gain new authority, respect, and responsibility. We take on a new mission: to make change on a larger scale for students. However, we lose opportunities for close relationships with our students. We find our time frittered away by things that we know are not central to our mission. We become responsible for factors that can seem beyond our control. We make a trade, gaining greater influence in the school community as a whole but losing the ability to witness, up close, individual students making long- and short-term strides in their learning—within curriculum and within life. We miss collaborating with our colleagues, because there are fewer leaders in schools, and we find ourselves eating lunch over our keyboards, in solitude. We feel as though our time is not our own.

When we gain something, we lose something. Or do we?

It's true that we give up a great deal when we change roles after years of teaching. However, we don't have to give up everything. We don't have to give up our commitment to learning, or students, or education. We don't have to give up our dedication to teachers or the practices we've embraced.

Roland Barth (1990) of the Harvard Principals' Center coined the phrase *head learner* to describe what the principalship could and should be: school and district leaders making decisions with learning at their heart, leaders who never stop thinking about their learning or that of the students and professionals in their care, leaders who see their primary job as creating an environment where learning will thrive, not *because* they satisfy silly mandates sent to them from outside but *despite* these mandates. Barth's head learner supports learning that is home-grown and authentic, much more powerful than the compliance that school leaders are, more than ever, pressured into today. How prophetic of Roland Barth to have this vision starting in the 1980s, some thirty-plus years before we ever muttered the words *Common Core*.

This book is an invitation to you to be the type of school or district leader who doesn't corner students and teachers into compliance, but creates an environment in which learning is simply a way of life. This book is a road map to help you figure out how to let learning guide the many, many decisions you make each day in your work. This book is a reminder to you about just why you came into teaching in the first place—to inspire others to discover and to better themselves.

It is my hope that this book will help you hold on to being a teacher and a learner, even while you occupy the principal's office.

The Changing Role of the Principalship

From the Colonial period through much of the nineteenth century, schools were run by people called "principal teachers" or "head teachers." Usually men, these were members of the family who owned the school or were the teachers favored by school boards. Sometimes they were the only ones in the school who had experience and formalized training in teaching itself or were the only ones who wanted to take on the extra responsibility of running the school. Starting in the late nineteenth century, schools began to take on the administrative structure we know today. That's when the term *principal* changed from being an adjective to being a noun. Its overall meaning also changed when it was separated from the noun it had modified, *teacher*. Principals throughout the twentieth century had less and less direct teaching responsibility and more and more managerial work. It seems that when talented teachers with a call to leadership took on this role, they became further and further removed from the work they truly loved. The further removed they became, the greater the divide became between their understanding of the daily happenings in the classroom and with the teachers in those classrooms. Jim Montesano, the superintendent who first took a chance on me as a principal, often referred to the distinction made by Steven Covey between what is *urgent* and what is *important* as a principal. There are many urgent matters that a principal addresses: safety, student discipline, and other issues that often come out of the blue and have an almost immediate deadline. However, they are not to be confused with important matters, which tend to revolve around the human parts of our work: building relationships, ensuring good learning for students and teachers, staffing our schools, and other projects that usually take quite a long time to take hold. When we remind ourselves that *principal* is an adjective, we can lead our schools as head learners, who create environments of engagement, not simply compliance.

Establishing the Learner's Mindset

We can begin to take on the role of "head learner" and reclaiming the principalship by establishing a learning mindset. This book offers suggestions for how to do that. Each chapter explores a different way of keeping in touch with learning by connecting with others.

Chapter 1 gives options for connecting with other principals and learning alongside them.

Chapter 2 explores ways to connect with teachers in the classroom, teaching alongside them by taking on instructional coaching.

Chapter 3 addresses the connection between learning and the many managerial decisions principals must make.

Chapter 4 connects the professional development and evaluative aspects of the principal's job to get the most out of observation and evaluation.

Chapter 5 discusses how to connect teachers, students, and community members through the use of learning themes and teaching metaphors.

Chapter 6 offers practical ways in which you can connect with and nurture your own learning life.

Each Day . . .

Learning—ours, our students', and our teachers'—touches not only every aspect of our work but every moment of our day. The chapters that follow will take us on a journey together. Before we get into the specifics of networking, coaching, managing, building community, and evaluating, let's consider some daily habits that will help a focus on instruction take root in our work.

Make yourself a witness to learning. I don't know about you, but I find that if I work on administrative tasks for fifteen minutes or six hours, the work is never really done. If we consistently make that work our top priority, it leaves us disconnected from the school. Instead, plan to leave the office and put yourself in the presence of learning every day. Whether it's a kindergartner finally figuring out how to tie a shoe, a middle school student figuring out a new theory about *The Giver*, or a teacher with fifteen years of experience learning a new way to differentiate a very difficult topic in math, make sure you're there to see it happen. Then think about it. The following questions help me to consider both the individual instances of learning as well as larger trends in our school:

- Who did the learning? What was learned?
- What did the learner (or a teacher or a partner) do right before to help make the learning stick?
- How did this experience affect the learner?
- How is this transferrable to other situations?

Gossip productively. When you witness learning, gossip about it—in a positive way. You might say to another teacher, the nurse, anyone who will listen: "I saw Joey finally figure out the nines in multiplication." "Sadie and Matthew just had the best conversation about their book." "Lorraine just had the coolest conference with a student." This spreads excitement and helps teach others about how things are learned. It also helps all of the adults in your school to see that you value learning, not just compliance or orderliness. It sets the scene for the work you'll be doing as an instructional leader.

Humble yourself. This isn't the same as embarrassing yourself. It's just about reminding yourself that you don't have all the answers and that you shouldn't put that kind of pressure on yourself. If you're not humble, you can't learn. If you can't learn, you can't really teach. If you can't teach, you certainly can't lead teachers.

Sometimes I think the great recipe for learning leadership is to have a learner's soul, a teacher's heart, a staff developer's mind, and an administrator's hand. Let's focus on the learner's heart: it's always ready to take in something new, and possibly let go of something old. Being an imperfect, malleable person brings with it the need to be humble, and that can be hard when you're the leader.

Here are a few ideas on how to remain humble, even as a leader.

- *Repeat a mantra.* Find something that you'll say each morning as you get ready for work that reminds you how important it is to be humble.

- *Place an artifact of humility in your office.* This might be a picture, a poster, or a word that you will see during the day that will remind you to approach your work with a learner's mind.

- *Thank others for what you have learned from them.* When you consider all of the ways that you learn in your work, you'll find that you're likely learning from everyone in the school: students, teachers, staff, and parents. When you find yourself learning from others, thank them, saying, "Let me tell you what I just learned from you. . . ."

- *Make compliments and thank-yous collaborative.* When someone compliments you or thanks you, they're offering you an opportunity to build community with them by complimenting or thanking them back. Rather than simply accepting compliments or thanks, look for places where you can honestly show how something is a collaborative effort. For example, if a teacher compliments you on a good all-school assembly, thank him for the work he did to prepare students for it so that they were ready to join in.

- *Create a question board.* Have a question board in your office, where you'll post something you're trying to learn through your work. When you find the answer, post a new question.

- *When someone says something you disagree with, go with it.* People will undoubtedly say things that you disagree with. Live with the idea for an hour, a day, a week. Try to find what's strong about their idea. You may not change your mind, but this exercise may help you to see others' perspectives more clearly.

- *Set a learning goal each year.* A principal I know once said that he makes a point of learning something new each year. One year, it was skiing. Another year, it was learning Spanish. Setting these types of goals starts with the admission that you don't know everything, which fosters humility.

- *Ask questions.* Ask students, teachers, other staff members to teach you about things. Some of these might be about education, and some might not.

- *Compliment and ask about process.* Say to someone, "I just saw you _____. How did you do that?" You might also ask why, but be careful not to look like you're asking them to justify. Instead, take on a curious tone to convey that you're genuinely interested in learning.

- *Ask teachers (or students) to name what they're thinking.* When we do things with automaticity, we don't stop to think about our thinking. When observing or coaching a teacher, stop after a particularly rich teaching moment, and ask, "What are you thinking right now?" This open-ended reflection can give you and the teacher a learning moment to share.

- *Ask people to teach you how to do things.* My secretary is so adept at technology. She's helped me figure out my GPS, program an iPad, and navigate Google Docs. Think of things you need help with, and find others who can help you figure them out.

Choosing Not to Give It All Up

When I was a staff developer at the Teachers College Reading & Writing Project, I worked with Elizabeth, the principal of a large elementary school in Ohio. Elizabeth was involved. She cared. She had something positive to say about every teacher we discussed. She seemed to know most of the 900 students in her school. She knew the newest picture books. She knew about teaching in a writing workshop. She talked about specific goals she had in mind for her teachers.

I mentioned to her literacy coach that Elizabeth must be great to work with. She nodded, and tears seemed to creep to the corner of her eyes. "Yes," she said. "She gets it. It's like having a teacher in the principal's office."

She took on leadership, but chose not to give up being a teacher at heart. I worked with Elizabeth for four years, and there were times she told me about how hard it is to keep the teacher in you alive. It's so easy to be caught up in the administration, the management, the discipline, the politics, all of which she had taken on as a principal, but she made the conscious choice to remember every one of her students' names, and three things about each of them (yes, all 900 of them!).

This book is an effort to make us all a little bit more like Elizabeth—not ready to give up the teacher inside us, just because we've taken on something new. Schools need leaders who make their teachers feel like there's a teacher in the principal's office, with just as much love for teaching and learning as they had when they started their careers. Make the word *principal* an adjective again. Join me, Head Learner, on the journey of reclaiming the principalship in the name of learning!

Chapter 1

GET SMARTER WITH A PROFESSIONAL NETWORK

The scene is an elementary school library. Thirty-one principals, assistant principals, and curriculum supervisors—all at different phases of their careers, all at different points in their implementation of balanced literacy and the use of makerspaces (the focuses of the day)—are talking in small groups about conferring. "Conferring is definitely the hardest part," says Margy, a K–5 principal and former district staff developer. Mike, the principal of a 3–6 school, nods his head in agreement. His eyebrows curl up in hearing Margy's words. Mike has just started reading and writing workshops in his school, and he's been particularly frustrated with the complexity of conferences.

Melissa Signore is the principal of the school that is the meeting place this day. As she sips her coffee, she tells Janelle, the director of special services from another district, "Conferring doesn't get easy overnight." Janelle chimes in, saying, "It's a struggle, but my teachers are saying it's a way of totally differentiating, and they love that."

Middle school principal Matt shares how his learning stance has both changed the energy in his school and renewed his own love for teaching and learning and leadership. Steve, who had considered leaving the principalship because the administrative work had just become too overwhelming, talks about how he now has new love for his work. Laura tells how the class she adopted as a coach had the highest test scores in the district. She's not sure if it's just because she was there, but she notes her teachers view her differently now, and she's thankful for it. One assistant principal had to take a personal day to be here: his superintendent sees assistant principals as "managing a building," not fostering learning. The superintendent didn't see the value in this type of learning day, but the assistant principal had already seen the power of this work in action, and he didn't want to miss it.

This was one of five meetings during the year where learning leaders in our area gather to learn from one another, from teachers and students, and from their own stories of creating positive school culture through leadership. Like all dedicated communities, our group started organically, gathering around an idea during a very teachable moment.

I was leading some summer professional development (PD) about teaching writing with a group of fifteen principals. The excitement around the teaching of writing was high, but we were afraid that September, with its scheduling and discipline, with its bullying and lunchtimes, with its security drills and endless meetings, would drain the momentum we had built up over the last four days. We decided to make a pact to stick together to maintain the learning we had enjoyed and gather together throughout the year at each other's schools. It was reminiscent of the networks of principals and other leaders I had worked with in New York City as a staff developer at the Teachers College Reading and Writing Project.

We decided to do it. All in! And the New Jersey Literacy Leaders Network was born.

Word spread quickly that principals were learning together and working in classrooms, conferring with kids, getting their hands dirty. They were leaving their hives five times a year to do this. The numbers quickly grew: people were curious at first, then involved, then engaged. Five years into the journey, over 150 head learners from urban, suburban, and rural communities have signed on, committed to study good learning with each other. We don't see all of them at every meeting, but they're all part of the community, and welcome to join when they can.

Why Network?

It's lonely in the principal's office—lonely, if you don't count all the mandates and new demands that make their home in the office with you. It's even lonelier if you're the only principal at your own level or if your district has a highly competitive culture among its schools. How can principals keep up with the increasing demands in work that can feel more and more isolating, pushing you into a corner?

The answer is to make yourself less lonely. Push yourself out of the corner, addressing the new demands head-on, joining forces with others who will help you take them on. One of the ancient secrets of leadership and learning is to surround yourself with others with whom you can learn. Creating a learning group of leaders who are dedicated to building a knowledge base in curriculum is a great way to rekindle the spirit of learning—the very spirit that led most of us into education in the first place!

Liam is the assistant principal of an elementary school, that is pioneering a new model of instruction. I invited one of his teachers to a workshop on a day when there were no students in school. All we would need is for his teacher to have one day off. "You're asking the wrong guy," he told me. "I don't have the authority to sign off on that."

Anne is a principal friend of mine, who invited me to visit her school for a day. She wanted to move her school into a more student-driven approach to teaching. "We can have a demonstration lesson in one of your classrooms, and the other teachers from that grade can join us," I suggested. "Well, I'll have to check with the teachers' union," she said.

Liam and Anne's stories are symptomatic of something that is happening in schools today—more and more principals are acting as administrators, not leaders. *Administrators enact and manage the vision of others. Leaders create vision with the help of others and lead toward that vision.* If we feel powerless, like Liam and Anne, we can't accomplish anything, and we can't make progress.

When leaders come together to study good teaching, they form their thinking together. When they coauthor a vision that they can carry together across time and across district lines, they find safety in numbers and a new depth of thinking in a learning community.

> *This network not only helps me build capacity in my teachers, but also bolsters my skills. It allows me to understand how teachers feel when implementing a new practice . . . uncertainty, risk-taking, and trepidation. It has been a motivating, helpful experience . . . redefining my role as an instructional leader.*
>
> **—Sheldon Silver, principal of East Brook Elementary School, Park Ridge, New Jersey**

There is a very practical side to networking also. Principals share resources, posting articles and sharing new ideas, online and in person. They send SOS messages the last week of summer vacation when they are hit with a last-minute resignation. When they find themselves facing a crisis—their first death of a parent, for example—they have a huge group they can turn to for advice and support. They ask each other for honest opinions about programs they've heard about—are they really all they're cracked up to be? They band together to share expenses for PD and other opportunities for their schools.

Forming Your Community

Just as with any community, you must decide on a focus. Our network dealt with literacy, but really, the community you create can be focused around anything related to teacher and student learning. It can be subject-specific (literacy, mathematics, STEM, character education, etc.). It can be about other topics within teaching and learning (special education, meaningful integration of technology, assessment-driven teaching, the development of innovative learners, etc.).

Questions That Will Help You Find a Community Focus

1. What learning topic do I want to explore?
2. What areas do I have some expertise in that I could share?
3. Who are some principals in other districts I'd like to study with?
4. What strengths do I admire in other principals I know?

Once you have your topic, you need to broaden your audience. You don't need a large number to start. Just think of who you'd like to invite to a study group on a topic. Your next step will be to start planning your face-to-face time together.

One caveat: try to avoid the involvement of money. When you ask for money for a study group, it can cause distrust and will immediately limit the number of people who can attend, especially those who do not feel that they have the power to approve a financial request.

The first day of your study group can be an exciting one. Of course, there are some logistical details to consider and communicate: parking, a meeting room, refreshments. You'll also need to consider which classroom(s) you'll be visiting with your guests, and how you'll frame these visits for your own staff, who will undoubtedly be curious about the visitors.

What Do Network Meetings Look Like?

See if this sounds familiar: You are heading into a meeting about a topic that is important to you. You've carved out precious time to make this meeting happen. You're well prepared. You have lots to discuss. And then . . . things get off track. The other leaders become fascinated with an interesting theoretical point and never get back to the real-world issues you've gathered to address. The parent is more interested in discussing the school lunch options than their child's trouble in school. The superintendent is so passionate about a new leadership book she just read that you never get to discuss the burning issues that you need help with *right now*.

It has been very helpful to meet with other administrators outside our district to share ideas about supporting teachers. I have gotten some good ideas about materials and structures to use for study groups with teachers. I have also had some good ideas from other administrators about differentiated ways to support teachers. Hearing other administrators tell their stories of launching a new initiative . . . adds to my knowledge base. I can learn from their successes and challenges.

—Jeanine Nostrame, principal of Ridge Ranch Elementary School, Paramus, New Jersey

We all know how it feels to have our hopes of a productive, useful meeting dashed. Our hopes for a resolution fall away, and we're left feeling frustrated about lost time and effort. Here are a few ground rules for keeping your meetings focused on what matters: student learning.

- Whenever possible, *make sure your face-to-face meetings are in a school*. Schools are sanctified ground for learning. Being in a school gives you the opportunity to work with students and teachers directly and to see the environments you'll be discussing. Nothing is more real than that, and that authenticity will add power to your study.

- *Have a predictable structure* for your leaders' group that includes time to work together, time to observe, and time to interact with students in a classroom setting. Time spent in classrooms interacting with students and teachers helps ground the day in authentic practice. It's so easy to become theoretical in our discussions (especially if we ourselves have been out of the classroom for a number of years), but testing out our learning in the classroom keeps it very real. It also adds layers of credibility to our work in the eyes of those we serve!

Figure 1.1 shows the meeting structure that has worked for our leadership network over the last several years.

The next few pages explain how each of these components works. Then, we'll discuss how to lay the groundwork for these meetings and how to prepare for them, as well as how to follow-up after meetings.

FIGURE 1.1

LEADERSHIP NETWORK MEETING STRUCTURE		
Time Estimates	**Component**	**What This Looks Like . . .**
Shortly after the school day begins	Arrival	Participants arrive after the morning rush is over.
20 minutes	Morning chat	The hosting principal gives some background on the school, including a description of how the school has been addressing the group's central topic and what progress has been made.
60–90 minutes	Group work	The group members work together to explore an aspect of their central topic in depth.
60 minutes	Lab site	The group members visit a classroom to observe or interact with students, grounding their work in the group in actual interactions with students.
60 minutes	Lunch	Order in and use the time for talk that's a little less formal.
30 minutes	Learning visits	Participants walk through the hallways and spontaneously visit classrooms.
30 minutes	End-of-day gathering	Participants reflect on their learning and offer feedback. This often includes feedback to the host principal.

Arrival

The work you do ahead of your meeting will make arrival go smoothly. Let people know in advance via email when to arrive, where to park, where to report in the school, what to bring, and what to expect from the day.

Morning Chat

The hosting principal meets with the group to share the story of his or her leadership, paying particular attention to the focus of the group. Telling the school's implementation story, no matter whether the school is just beginning the process or building on years of work, is a powerful way for participants to get the complete vision of making positive change. The host principal can explain how he or she allocated space, time, money, and people to create growth, and can share the struggles along the way.

Group Work

This time is set aside for group members to work together, tightly focused on their central topic. During our first meeting, we use this time to plan an overall agenda together. After that, our intentions are set, and we typically use one of the following structures during our group work time:

PD in a Box. The facilitator runs a PD activity that participants can take back to their schools and implement right away during faculty meetings or team meetings. If someone in the network is particularly strong at something that would be helpful for the group, invite him or her to lead this session. In our group, we've had success with the following suggestions:

- Share a PowerPoint or Prezi presentation on a topic of mutual interest that principals can take back and use right away.

- Work in groups to analyze a batch of student work: sorting the work to find patterns, and then brainstorming how teachers might move these students along the continuum of proficiency.

- Discuss an article or video clip. Participants can read or view the material ahead of time.

- Demonstrate a transferrable lesson about a topic that is applicable across grades, such as growth mind-set or student autonomy. Participants can replicate these lessons with their teachers who, in turn, may want to replicate them in their classrooms.

Book Studies. Invite participants to read a few chapters of a relevant professional book before the meeting, and then discuss the content. If people seem to be summarizing the book, or if the discussion turns theoretical, bring the talk back to how the content can be implemented right away. Give yourself and your group permission to abandon a book if you're not seeing results. The book is only a tool. If the tool isn't helping, you don't need to use it.

Round Table Talks. Ask participants to come prepared to discuss a central topic, one that is important in their work. The facilitator transcribes the conversation and sends the notes out to all participants afterward, highlighting important takeaways for how to implement the ideas shared.

Lab Site

The lab site is the visit to a classroom where participants will have the chance to work directly with students. Students will be learning. Your guests will be learning. You will be learning, too. Working together with students, trying out the teaching and refining it, is perhaps the most authentic best practice.

There are many ways to structure your time within the lab site. Lab sites can be demonstration-oriented (one person models and voices over what he or she is doing, while the others observe and take notes). They can be guided practice (the facilitator sets up a scaffolded activity, which participants practice with individual students or small groups). They can be explorations (everyone tries out the teaching in small groups or with individual students and reports back to the group). They can be a mix of all of these.

How you choose to structure lab sites really depends on your level of experience, the level of experience of the participants, and the level of implementation of whatever it is you're studying within the host school. The way I structure lab sites reflects what I learned from and with colleagues during my years as a staff developer with the Teachers College Reading and Writing

A NOTE FOR YOUR FIRST MEETING: SETTING A MUTUAL AGENDA

Starting off with a mutual plan sets your group up for collaboration and success. These protocols will help ensure that participants have a voice in setting the agenda. The agency and ownership created by this practice on the first day will help strengthen the community, which may help people feel motivated to return on subsequent days.

Agenda-Setting Option 1: Sorting Ideas

- **Table Setting:** A facilitator explains the overarching topic and briefly discusses why this topic matters to the children in our schools.
- **Brainstorming:** Participants write their thoughts or questions about the topic on sticky notes.
- **Calibration:** Participants share their notes with the whole group, sorting them into categories, and then naming the major categories that have emerged.
- **Questioning:** Participants work in small groups around each category, taking the ideas found in the notes and turning them into an open-ended essential question for each category.
- **Agenda Setting:** Group members post these questions and decide what their work in a classroom will be that day.

Agenda-Setting Option 2: Graffiti Wall

- **Setup:** The facilitator posts four or five pieces of chart paper around the room with questions or statements about the topic in the center of each.
- **Table Setting:** A facilitator explains the overarching topic and briefly discusses why this topic matters to the children in our schools.
- **Brainstorming:** Participants walk around and comment on each statement with a magic marker. Each person comments on each sheet.
- **Calibration:** Participants circulate again, this time to comment on each other's comments, again writing on each sheet.
- **Questioning:** Participants work in small groups around each sheet, taking the ideas found on the pages and turning them into an open-ended, essential question.
- **Agenda Setting:** Group members post these questions and decide what their work in a classroom will be that day.

Project. You may have other methods in mind. The only rule is that participants *must* have time to actively engage with students.

I also encourage giving participants guide sheets for use in lab sites, something I learned from Kathleen Tolan, former Deputy Director of the Teachers College Reading and Writing Project. Kathleen was a master at designing and using guide sheets to scaffold learning for teachers and principals in lab sites. Guide sheets help participants to see the structure of the lesson and to capture their own thinking during the lesson. We'll discuss guide sheets more in Chapter 2 as a tool for coaching. In Figure 1.2 (see pages 11 to 16), you can see a more complex guide sheet for a lab site I facilitated on workshop teaching. The lab site in this plan is differentiated because of the variety of levels of experience of the participants. Before the lab site began, I asked participants to sort themselves into "strand A" (participants who have more experience with workshop) and "strand B" (participants who are relative new to workshop). I also asked them to find a partner within their strand. Not all guide sheets need to be this intricate!

Lunch

We usually order lunch in the morning so that it's there in time. Sometimes, people see lunch as a time to leave without too much distraction, so you might want to have some time devoted to an interesting topic to keep them around. Also, you might schedule a late lunch so that you can tackle as much content before it as possible.

Learning Visits

Learning visits are walk-throughs of the school. Participants gather data to provide feedback for the host principal. The focus of the visits could be something that the school is already studying, so that the observations can be more visible and productive. You may choose to use learning visit guide sheets, such as those found in Chapter 3, or you may want to use a guide sheet like the one in Figure 1.3 (see page 17), a more open-ended model that does not use a specific lens for the visit. Each person brings his or her own experiences, biases, and interests to this type of visit, so working without a lens allows for a more diverse discussion afterward.

FIGURE 1.2

MODEL LAB SITE GUIDE SHEET

Spring Hill Elementary School
Second-Grade Reading, December 12, 2016

Please work with your partner in the lab site.

> *I teach the minilesson, voicing over what I'm teaching. So, for example, I might interrupt what I'm saying to students to turn to the adult participants and make a comment like, "This is the connection, where I'm setting the context. Notice how it's just me talking, and that at the end, I'm stating my teaching point." The participants in strand A watch and take notes with a mentoring lens, writing down things they might point out to a novice teacher. The participants in strand B write down some of the essential parts of the minilesson that they themselves are studying.*

Minilesson

Tom will teach a minilesson. If you and your district are new to workshop teaching, follow strand A. If you and your district are familiar with workshop teaching, follow strand B.

Strand A: Fill in this table as though you were pointing out something about teaching structure, content, or management to a novice teacher.

Part	Minilesson Structure	Minilesson Content	Minilesson Management
Connection			
Teach			
Active Involvement			
Link			

continues

Strand B Fill in this table.

Part	Approximate Time	Who's Talking?	What Else Do You Notice?
Connection			
Teach			
Active Involvement			
Link			

I model for a table of students the teaching of an "always question". Participants note the topic of nonfiction book that is discussed and the questions that a reader can always ask when reading about that topic. Participants are then given the chance to try it out again at other tables.

Table Conferences

Watch Tom as he approaches a group of students and teaches them another type of "always question" (a question that a reader can *always* ask when reading nonfiction books about a certain topic).

Topic	Question

Go to another group, and teach the group another always question from this list.

continues

If the group is reading another topic, work with a partner to brainstorm another always question.

When Reading About . . .	You Can Always Ask . . .
Animals	How does the animal use its body to survive? How is this animal like or different from other animals? How does this animal adapt to its habitat?
Technology	How does this invention make life easier? Why was this invented?
Places	How is this place like where I live? How is it different?
Cultures	How is this culture like mine? How is it different? What important things do people in this culture do? Why?
Famous People	What hardships did this person overcome? Why is the world different because of this person?
Events	How did this event change the world?

Here, I divide the group. Notice how the parts of the conference are broken down for participants with very supportive thinking prompts. After each part (research, compliment, teach), participants go off to replicate that part of the conference with students in the class, while I coach them. This helps them work out the conference, part by part.

Conferring

Strand A Confer with students. Use all you know about conferring to teach your students. (Start at the *Even More Conferring* section.)

Strand B Gather at the meeting area with Tom. Watch as he confers with a student. Try to figure out what he might compliment the student on and what he might teach.

Possible Compliments	Possible Teaching Points

continues

More Conferring

Go to a student with your partner. Partner 1, be the teacher. Partner 2, be the timekeeper. Use the following questions to ask strategy-oriented, open-ended questions. Record possible compliments and teaching points (not related to mechanics). At the end of four minutes, decide on one compliment and pay it. Then go to another child and switch roles. We will meet at the carpet in ten minutes.

Open-Ended Questions	Follow-Up Questions
How's it going?	What do you mean?
What are you working on today as a reader/writer?	Please say more about that.
What are you thinking about in your work right now?	Please show me a place where that happens.
What's going well for you?	How do you know?
What's giving you difficulty in your work today?	Why do you do that?
What do you do when _____?	
Last time, you were working on _____. How's that going?	
I noticed you were _____. Can you talk about that?	

Student 1 _____

Possible Compliments	Possible Teaching Points

Student 2 _____

Possible Compliments	Possible Teaching Points

continues

Even More Conferring

Strand A Pay the compliment and teach the student the most relevant teaching point. (Use the boxes under the *Words to Use* section to organize your teaching.)

Strand B Return to the meeting area and watch Tom as he pays the compliment and teaches the teaching point.

Part	What Tom Says
Compliment	
State the Teaching Point	
Demonstration	
Coaching/Guided Practice	
Link	

Strand B Return to the students from earlier and finish their conferences, using the boxes under the *Words to Use* section to organize their teaching.

Partner 1:

Part	Words to Use
Compliment	
State the Teaching Point	
Demonstration	
Coaching/Guided Practice	
Link	

continues

Partner 2:

Part	Words to Use
Compliment	
State the Teaching Point	
Demonstration	
Coaching/Guided Practice	
Link	

All participants listen to student partnerships talk to one another.

Partner Work

We will transition into partner work. Listen in on one partnership and find something to compliment them on.

Student Names: _____ and _____

Compliment: _____

Share

Jot down something you noticed someone doing well today that could be used to create a share at the end of the workshop.

FIGURE 1.3

RESEARCHING OUR SCHOOLS		
Location/Teacher	**What You Notice**	**What That Makes You Think**

Have participants walk through the classrooms with a partner. Partners who work together in the *same* district can start off conversations they can carry back to their home district. Partners who work in *different* districts can help one another think about nuances that go beyond their own personal experience. No matter where participants are from, they should be careful to avoid judgmental language (even if it's positive!), which can hinder them from noticing what's *behind* what they're seeing.

And what about you? As the facilitator of the day, you also walk through, floating between partnerships so that you can help to point out things that visitors may not otherwise notice. Coach them to notice and think about what's going on around them.

Words to Help Coach During a Learning Visit

- Did you notice _____? Why do you think that's happening?
- Did you see/hear what that teacher/student just said/did?
- Another partnership just commented on this. What do you think about that?
- The host principal was telling me about this. Let me explain.

Engaging in the visit by talking to students or teachers can yield important information. During one such visit, I visited a second-grade class that was working in writing workshop. At this age, students tend to write on different types of paper to account for the diversity of student development in the area of writing. Indeed, students *were* writing on different types of paper. It looked just right! I pointed that out to the visiting principals who were studying how to differentiate in writing instruction. However, I wanted to dig a little deeper to see the function behind the form.

I approached Samantha, who was working very hard on the nonfiction book she was writing. Playing the naive adult, I said, "Samantha, I notice that you're writing on paper with lots of lines, and your friend across from you is writing on paper with a big box [presumably for drawing] and not so many lines. Why is that?" Samantha said, "It's because I'm on Chapter 3, and this is Chapter 3 paper, and he's on Chapter 2, and that's Chapter 2 paper." It was a surprising answer. The teacher was not actually differentiating according to student needs, something that we'd want to discuss afterward.

After about 30–40 minutes of walking through the school, everyone returns to the meeting room to share their noticings. Because the participants took such an active part in walking around, they need to have an active role in driving the discussion.

One way to structure this discussion is by talking about the strengths observed. Use stems that name what was seen, and then explain why that's perceived to be a strength. For example, "I noticed that there was lots of student work on the wall. That's important, because it makes students feel a great deal of agency and ownership in the room."

Although it's not required to talk about perceived weaknesses as a group, visitors tend to bring up some of their doubts. Most people are respectful and sensitive to phrasing these queries constructively in the form of a question or a wonder. For example, "I noticed that students in second grade weren't using differentiated paper. I wonder why that might be."

You might track some of the trends the group is discussing on the board, synthesizing them as you're writing. Keep in mind what the overarching theme of the day is, and see if you can relate people's observations to this theme.

Try to phrase the discussion in terms of takeaways. Talk to principals about how they can apply what they're seeing. If something is clearly going well in the school, ask the principal to elaborate on how it was created. Remind participants that they too *can* get there if they budget their time, money, and human resources appropriately. If something is a perceived weakness, talk about next steps, including PD or allocation of funds. Takeaways help people see hope and possibilities.

End-of-Day Gathering

When your day is over, think about how you'll link the day's work to the work of the next meeting day. What work will participants do in their own schools to further their study? Remember that everyone can be doing slightly different work between your first and second meetings. You might frame this part of the meeting like this:

Today, we studied _____. How will you:

- *Use this in your work with teachers?*
- *Look for this in your own school?*
- *Find more evidence of it in your work?*

You might also ask principals to partner up with one another to check in with each other. These pairings offer the chance for further networking, based on needs.

Between Meetings

Your network is up and running! You've laid the groundwork for some exciting study around leadership. You've probably begun to make some new professional friends or added new layers of friendship to colleagues you've already known. How do you keep the momentum going so that your experience is not just another one-stop workshop? How do you nurture the sense of community that will lead to the greatest success for your group? A few suggestions for following up between meetings:

Send thank-you emails. Email the host principal and any teachers who were involved in making the day successful, naming strengths you saw during your visit. For example:

> *Dear (lab site teacher),*
>
> *Thank you for opening up your classroom to us! We learned so much from you and your students. Many of our visiting principals commented on (name a few strengths). I know it's hard to have company in your space, but by opening your doors, you've helped thousands of kids you don't even know. Thanks so much!*
>
> *—Tom*

Send any notes from the meeting out in a group email. This lets participants see each others' email addresses, which gives them the ability to follow up with each other or to reach out with a question or request for help.

Plan your next meetings. Map out where the next few meetings will be. Your meetings should be held in a location that's convenient to all. Plan according to levels of experience in the topic you're studying. For example, if your network is studying balanced literacy, select host schools that have varying amounts of experience in this type of teaching.

Planning for Meetings

A well-planned day makes for the greatest success. About two weeks before your meeting, schedule a face-to-face, on-site planning session with the principal who will be hosting the next meeting. Here are some things to address during your visit.

Figure out logistics. Ask about parking, arrival and dismissal times, refreshments, check-in procedures, and anything else that participants will need to know.

Identify a theme. Ask the host principal what he or she is proud of that relates to your group's central topic. Some of our principals have highlighted celebration, consistency, student-driven instruction, or the role of conversation in instruction. These can become anchors for the lab site, learning visits, or any part of the day.

Talk about the school's implementation of the network's topic. Ask the host principal to explain where the school is in implementing the focus work. Talk about successes, struggles, and next steps. These can be taught into throughout the day, and they'll be at the heart of the morning chat on your meeting day.

Decide on a lab site. Work with the principal to decide on a lab site classroom. It should be a room where the teacher is comfortable having visitors, where the classroom management is stable, and where the work is going well.

Talk to the lab site teacher. Clarify that you and the other participants are school leaders who are hoping for a chance to sharpen their instructional game and that you are not acting as observers or evaluators. Talk about the logistics of the time you'll be in and where they will be in their curriculum. Explain exactly what you have in mind for your time in the teacher's classroom.

Talk to the lab site students. Visit the classroom and explain to the students that visitors will be coming. You might also want to establish some of your own management expectations with them. Indeed, it can be unusual for many adults to visit their classroom. Ask them to stay focused on the teaching and learning, not the crowd. For example, I might say to students:

> *How many of you like to work with a friend when you're learning something new, like a sport or a musical instrument? Well, teachers and principals do the same. We think teaching can be challenging, and we like to work with each other, too. So, I called Mr. _____ and said we need a class of hard workers and good listeners to work with, and he said, "Have I got the class for you!"*
>
> *Let's make some rules for our work together. I'm going to promise you that when you talk to me, I won't interrupt you. I'm going to promise you that when you talk to me, I'll look at you and think about what you're saying. I promise you that when you talk to me, I won't let other things around me distract me. I'd like to ask you to promise the same things back to me. Is that fair?*
>
> *However, sometimes I'll interrupt myself, because that's allowed. I'll look up at the grown-ups and say, "Principals, blah, blah, blah, blah, blah." That's a signal to you to sit quietly for a minute. If you want to listen to me, you can, but you don't have to. It's just boring principal stuff. But then I'll turn back to you and say, "Third graders." That's a signal that you have to show me you're listening again. How do you show someone you're listening? Show me. Wow! You are good listeners!*

Finally, email your plans for the meeting to your network. Here's an example of what I sent out for a recent meeting of our network, including the agenda (see Figure 1.4):

From: *Tom Marshall dearmrmarshall@gmail.com*
Sent: *Wednesday, January 11, 2017 11:50 AM*
Subject: *our next meeting*

Hi everyone,

I'm attaching the agenda for our next meeting, on Monday, December 12th at Franklin School, 200 Mountain Road, Springfield, which is Lourdes' school and where Sue serves as curriculum director.

FIGURE 1.4

LITERACY LEADERS' NETWORK AGENDA

Franklin School, Springfield

Monday, December 12, 2016

The theme of this day's work is student-centeredness innovation!

8:45–9:15
Welcome and Snacks

- We'll introduce ourselves.
- We'll discuss the theme for the day.
- We'll discuss how things have gone since last year.

9:15–10:00
Engagement Versus Compliance

- We'll study a continuum of engagement for students and teachers.
- We'll plan out moves we can make as teachers and leaders to move those we serve across the progression.
- Tom will model some sample PD activities around this idea.

10:00–10:30
Engagement in Partnerships

- We'll study a learning progression on student partnerships.

10:30–11:30
Lab Site

- We will have a lab site in Lauren's second-grade unit of study on nonfiction reading.
- Tom will model a minilesson that will support students to start synthesizing in nonfiction reading.
- We'll confer with students about their nonfiction reading.
- Students will talk in clubs, and we'll use the partnership continuum to gauge their talking.
- We'll teach the students about conversation in their clubs.

11:30–12:00
Debriefing the Lab Site

12:00–12:45
Working Lunch: More on Partnerships

- We'll adapt the partnership continuum to reflect how grade-level teams might work together.
- We'll strategize how to use this continuum to push our teams to greater collaboration.

12:45–1:15
Conversation

- We'll study the role of talk in learning and prepare for our walk-throughs that will focus on talk.

1:15–2:00
Learning Visits

- We'll walk through the school, looking for snippets of learning talk, and then return to create a PD tool on this topic. (You won't want to miss this!)

2:00–2:30
Debriefing the Learning Visits

- We'll create a PD tool on conversation and school community that you can take back to use in your schools.

It promises to be a great day revolving around the idea of engagement!

You can park in the parking lot behind the school or in the gravel lot across the street from the school.

Please let me know if you are able to join us.

Tom

Making Time to Network

How do we add one more thing to our already quite full plates? It's easy to make the argument that you don't have time for one more thing. During my days at the Teachers College Reading and Writing Project, Lucy Calkins used to say to teachers who made this argument that, actually, time is *all* you have. Often, we don't have control over the financial resources that are allotted to us. Curriculum is often dictated. We can't choose the people who will work with us. However, to an extent, we can control how we use our time.

At the end of the summer, plot out your year. Start by plugging in all the holidays and times when school is closed. Then add the state-mandated items like testing and emergency drills. Follow that with district-level dates: the many meetings that you need to attend.

After all these items that are beyond your control are placed on your calendar, carve out time for your own learning. Find time to build partnerships and networks before your calendar fills with day-to-day events. If you don't nurture your own learning life, no one else will do it for you.

What If We Really Did Have Enough Guys?

Many in the field of literacy education would agree that the father of the process-oriented approach to teaching writing was Donald Graves (1930–2010). In *Teaching Day by Day: 180 Stories to Help You Along the Way* (2004), this master storyteller tells this tale:

> *In May of my junior year of college, something spontaneous occurred that I've never forgotten. Just after dinner on a warm spring evening*

my two roommates and I lazied our way back to the dormitory. One of us posed a simple question, "What could you do if you had enough guys?" My roommates were physics majors. One of them whipped out his slide rule and began calculating. "Yes!" he crowed. "If each person in the junior class had a hammer and chisel on a scaffold, we could dismantle the brick wall at the south end of the dormitory in about 45 minutes." We rolled on the grass with laughter.

Our laughter attracted a crowd, with more and more students stopping to listen to our wild speculations about what you could do if you had enough guys. When the laughter finally died down, everyone went back to the dorms to study. At midnight the bell signaling the beginning and end of classes suddenly started ringing. Spontaneously we poured from our rooms, half-dressed, still dressing, one question still on our minds, "What could you do if you had enough guys?"

We raced across the campus. Ten men picked up a VW bug and placed it on the library steps. Milk cans were hauled up flagpoles. The president's front door was nailed shut. Huge empty boiler tanks were rolled across lawns and placed in strategic locations to disrupt campus traffic. There was certainly power in numbers that night, the power to disrupt. At 2 a.m., we retired to our rooms. I've often pondered the events of that night, the surge of energy that brought with it the feeling of sudden power. What could happen if enough teachers and educators came together and speculated about what we could do for our children?

—(Graves 2004, 126)

Decades have passed since that eventful night on Don Graves' college campus, but Graves' question is still relevant. What could we do if we had enough guys? What could we do if as a group we showed everyone around us how powerful it is to give kids voice in their learning? What could we do if we didn't fear Common Core, and testing, and evaluation, but took control of them through good teaching? What if all of us learned together and put into practice what we learned? What if we found ways to empower ourselves, knowing there is safety in numbers and in good teaching? What if we all reached across the hallway to learn with our teachers, across our districts to learn with colleagues, across the nation with professional organizations, banding together with networks of professional friends? Imagine just what our schools would look like.

Angela Iskenderian, principal of Ann B. Smith School in Hillsdale, New Jersey, explains how having "enough guys" in our network has helped her school transition to balanced literacy over the past five years. "We all see the impact this network has made in our school community, especially with our students. Our boys and girls have developed as a community of readers. They have transitioned from basal readers to shopping for just-right books for a variety of genres in their classroom libraries; reading at their desks to reading around the room; writing in their workbooks to writing on their sticky notes to reflect on their reading; raising their hands and waiting to be called upon by their teacher to turning and talking to a partner; reading during scheduled reading periods to reading throughout the day, even at recess! This network and its educational leaders served as a change agent that made a powerful impact on teaching and learning for members of our school community."

What could we *all* do if we had enough guys?

Chapter 2

COACH TEACHERS TO IMPROVE STUDENT LEARNING

Taking what starts off as a short walk down the hallway, I'm stopped by a first-grade teacher who tells me about the amazing growth her most struggling reader has made and how the small-group interventions we had talked about seemed to do the trick. I only take a few more steps before a third-grade teacher pulls me aside to ask me about the learning progression she's developing to help her kids be more independent while revising their all-about books. Nodding my head at the end of an impromptu four-minute discussion, I give her a thumbs-up and take a few more steps before I'm stopped by two veteran teachers. They're grade partners who have just come out of a team meeting where they were stumped by the plans they're working on to start off a new unit on essays. They share their plans, and ask me how I might introduce this unit in a new way.

It's a good tired I feel as I head back down to the office. These short, crisp conversations are the ones I enjoy the most, and the ones that just might matter more than any other. Don't get me wrong. We still talk about difficult parents, scheduling changes, and the need to go over the specifics of an upcoming field trip. But these *learning* conversations happen more and more often, and it's all because of *coaching*.

As legendary basketball coach John Wooden once said, "A coach is someone who can give correction without causing resentment" (Abdul-Jabbar 2017, 63). How true this is in our work, as well. More and more, principals are taking on the role of instructional leader, influencing teacher practice and supporting student success by doing more than just evaluating their work. Evaluating is a *reactive* practice, where we compliment and critique a teacher's work after it is over. However, some of the greatest principals take an instructionally *proactive* stance to their work by supporting their teachers' practice all throughout the year.

In this chapter, we'll think about how you can coach your teachers, improving their practice without causing resentment. We'll look at how to carve out time for this vital leadership amidst all the demands of schedules, evaluations, discipline, parents, security, maintenance, and yes, lunch.

Coaching Versus Evaluation

During one of my literacy staff development visits to an elementary school, I remember one morning very well. I stopped in the classroom of Peter, an enthusiastic teacher. We were going to use his classroom as the demonstration lab site that morning. I asked him what he was working on.

The students were in a study of memoir writing, and they were excited to have read *When I Was Young in the Mountains* by Cynthia Rylant (1982). Thrilled to be using a new mentor text with his students, Peter set them up to do some writing that mirrored Rylant's voice. He planned to have students write with sentences that started with phrases like, "When I was young in…" over and over and over again. "What do you think?" he asked with a smile, anticipating my approval.

"It's nice that you're using a mentor text," I said. Then, I tried to explain that he could use the text differently. Instead of reproducing Rylant's words, we could help students to study and use her technique. This would allow students to use their own words and their own voice. I told Peter we could experiment with the lesson together when the other teachers arrived.

Two hours later, the room was filled with half a dozen teachers. I sat in the chair in the meeting area and taught the minilesson to the students. I asked Peter to demonstrate when we got to that part of the teaching. I stopped him after his first example, prompting the students, "Did you see what the teacher just did? He used Cynthia Rylant's words to get an idea for his own writing." Instead of letting Peter continue the long model he had in mind, I highlighted the move he was making and then turned the work over to the kids.

Shortly after the lesson, when we were sitting at the carpet with the teachers who had observed the lesson, Peter said, "I see now that my setting up the writing with these words was holding the students back." This is the kind of breakthrough we aim for in coaching. We help teachers to make discoveries and take risks, not just to implement what we tell them to do.

A fine line is drawn when the principal, who is the primary evaluator of classroom practice, acts as the coach. Coaches work with teachers when teachers are most vulnerable: teaching often less-than-polished lessons; working toward new competencies, but not yet mastering them. If we want teachers to take risks and grow, we must learn to notice things with a different lens—a coaching lens.

This is tricky work. You never really can separate yourself, leaving the evaluative part outside when you enter the classroom. Just the same, you never really abandon the coaching part of you when you enter a classroom, either. Part of instructional leadership is knowing when to let each part of you take the lead.

Let's say you walk into a classroom and see something that should be addressed. Maybe the students are not engaged in their work. You might notice that the charts on the wall are disorganized or all store-bought. There could be something in the physical arrangement of the room that needs to be fixed. How do you react? You might choose to let the *supervisor* in you react, telling the teacher what to change, implicitly or explicitly relying on your authority as principal to ensure that the change is made. Or, you might choose to let the *coach* in you react, treating the issue as a teachable moment. (See Figure 2.1.)

Let's examine these two different approaches in response to the same situation: You notice that all the anchor charts in Amy's classroom are in disarray on the walls. There seems to be no rhyme or reason to their organization. Science, writing, and math charts are lumped together. In fact, you notice that there are *too many* charts up on the wall, from all parts of the year, including charts that cover content that has already been mastered. (See Figure 2.2.)

Of course, there are times when an administrative response is necessary. A safety issue (blocking a fire egress, bad classroom management that becomes dangerous, the evolution of a disrespectful learning environment) needs to be handled with administrative response. When a teacher resists improvement even

FIGURE 2.1

DESCRIPTIONS OF SUPERVISOR/ADMINISTRATIVE RESPONSES VERSUS DESCRIPTIONS OF COACHING RESPONSES	
Supervisor/Administrative Responses	**Coaching Responses**
• Responses can be punitive or complimentary.	• Response withholds judgment.
• Effects take place immediately.	• Effects take a long time.
• Response creates compliance for the teacher, and does not engage the teacher in reflection.	• Response creates deeper knowledge and engagement for the teacher.
• Once the change is made, reflection stops.	• Once the change is made, new curiosity and conversations arise.
• Response may stifle future conversation between teacher and leader.	

after something has been coached and explored and reinforced, administrative response is required. These are instances when compliance is necessary. But when we employ the administrative response too quickly, we achieve only short-term compliance. The teacher might do as she was told quickly out of fear of repercussion, without really understanding *why* the practice was not the best one. In fact, the only lesson she might learn is to hide her practices from you. Not long-term, systemic change in teacher practice happens when we do this.

When we employ the coaching response, we have to allow the teacher time to explore and question the practice and allow ourselves time to work with the teacher on this practice. Making changes with coaching can take longer than simply issuing an administrative order. However, coaching, when done well, will have long-lasting effects.

When I see a less than desirable practice in the classroom and I'm considering which course to take—administrative or coaching—I ask myself the following questions:

- Why is the teacher doing this? Is it lack of knowledge, misinformed or dated practice, ignorance of what has been studied as a school community?

- Has the teacher been provided ample opportunities to know how alternatives might work?

EXAMPLES OF ADMINISTRATIVE RESPONSES VERSUS EXAMPLES OF COACHING RESPONSES

FIGURE 2.2

Administrative Response	Coaching Response
You very directly approach Amy and tell her that her charts are disorganized and that she should clean them up. You tell her that kids are probably feeling overwhelmed by all the information on the walls and that it's not as effective as if charts were organized according to subject area, and limited to what is being learned currently. You follow this up with a memo and tell her she has until Friday to make this right.	You make note of the arrangement of the charts on the wall, and you casually mention it to Amy. During subsequent visits, you coach Amy on just how students interact with charts to make them more independent in their work. In your coaching time, you layer in opportunities for Amy to see students acting with success when the charts are organized and relevant to current learning. You follow up with conversation and create a new common expectation.
Possible Outcome	**Possible Outcome**
The teacher might make the changes you noted, and might even make them relatively quickly, but these changes won't have much sticking power. The teacher will comply with your wishes, but won't be engaged with what you were trying to achieve, so she will make the same mistakes again, possibly even hiding concerns from you in the future.	The teacher will live with the idea for a sustained period of time, and the scaffolding, conversation, and exchange of ideas will engage the teacher in a deep thought process, at the end of which she will learn a lesson about teaching and learning that will spill over into other parts of her practice. This takes much longer, but its effects last much longer, too.

- Is the practice hindering student success? Is the practice getting in the way of the mission of the school or grade level?

- Is the practice dangerous? Is it an obstruction to student safety?

- Can this wait or do we need immediate compliance? Is the practice something that can be sustained through mere compliance, or is a deeper understanding necessary for the practice to be maintained in the long run?

Daniel Pink (2009) tells us in his work on motivation that carrots and sticks are effective when motivating people toward short-term goals. However, overuse of compliance-earning systems actually causes detriment to workplaces where the goal is creativity and innovation. When working with something as rich and three-dimensional as teaching and learning, we have to aim higher than just *compliance*—we need *engagement*, and that can be well achieved through coaching and other practices that might take just a little bit longer.

Getting Started: Who Are You as a Coach?

The first step in being a coaching principal is figuring out just what you have to offer. You might have expertise to offer in a certain subject area: literacy, math, science, social studies, technology, or integration of the arts. You might be interested in studying an aspect of teaching and learning that transcends discipline: classroom management, inquiry-based teaching, differentiating for support of special learners, developing partnerships, or fostering critical thinking skills. You could also just come in as an instructional coach, offering support in different areas for all your teachers.

Also bear in mind that you don't have to be the world's greatest authority in the area you choose. You just have to be willing to want to study this with your teachers, to be the head learner in that area. Often, teachers will appreciate the humble learning colleague more than the all-knowing guru.

Districts can be notorious for instituting almost "flavor of the month" initiatives that come and go each year. Don't align your coaching to something that teachers feel (or you feel) may not be around for the long haul. Choose something that you genuinely value and that will have a great impact on teacher practice and student achievement. This will give your work with teachers greater authenticity and power. Teachers know just how busy you are, and if they see you are interested enough in something to spend time coaching around it, they'll know it's important to you, and that it should be important to them.

Figure 2.3 will help you try on different aspects of teaching. These are very broad questions for you to reflect upon in determining an area of focus (if you want one) for you to coach teachers in.

FIGURE 2.3

POSSIBLE FOCUS FOR THE PRINCIPAL AS COACH

1. What experience or successes make you comfortable in this area?

2. What, if any, part of this focus are you not completely comfortable with?

3. Think of three very diverse teachers in your care. How would you be able to coach them in this area? How would working with them stretch you as a teacher and a leader?

4. What work could you do with a teacher in a classroom around this area (examples: modeling, coteaching, giving feedback)? What work could you do with a teacher outside the classroom in this area (examples: reflecting, reading/applying professional texts, engaging in work that is similar to the work students will try)?

5. What resources do you have at your disposal that might improve your own knowledge or the knowledge of a teacher in this area (examples: professional texts or videos, colleagues with experience in this area)?

Building Trust

So, wait a minute! My principal, who writes all my observations and evaluations, whose job it is to judge me, wants to come into my room and coach *me? Is this some secret way to get more information for my evaluation?*

Even when you have a great rapport with your teachers, this might be what some teachers initially feel when you tell them you want to coach them. These feelings might be warranted if they've never experienced coaching with a principal before, if they've only lived the evaluative dynamic between principal and teacher. And those feelings might be especially understandable if they've had adversarial relationships with previous administrators.

One thing you must do before the work of coaching really takes off is to gain teachers' trust. This may not happen overnight. The first step is transparency: announcing to your teaching staff that you'll be acting as a coach as part of an ongoing, collaborative process. This does not need a lot of fanfare, but it needs to be public. When I implemented a system of coaching at my school, I began by mentioning it in a staff meeting. I didn't explain the process at length or indicate that I thought that there was anything wrong with the current instruction in the school. Instead, I explained that I was looking for ways to be more involved with the students (which was completely true), and that I'd follow up with them individually with more information. Many of the teachers understood that I was eager to stay grounded in teaching, and those who weren't so trusting soon realized that this wasn't some "supervisory trick."

As a principal, you already know that there's no quick and easy plan for building trust. It takes consistent, genuine effort. Here are a few habits you can adopt to help the faculty members know that they can trust you:

- **Talk about your own experiences as a teacher,** especially the experiences that didn't go so well. It will remind teachers that you also have experience walking in their shoes and will let them know that you know you're not a perfect instructor.

- **Go into classrooms and ask to try out a lesson.** Teach in front of teachers and ask them for feedback. Sometimes, they'll be reluctant to offer critique, so ask them to watch with a certain lens, explicitly asking them to comment on what they might have done differently.

- **Buy them what they'll need to study with you**—professional texts or materials that are involved in whatever you're studying.

- **Do whatever you can to foster an environment in which teachers (and you!) collaborate, not compete, with each other.** All of your interactions with teachers each day contribute to this environment—each conversation in which you ask them about the work with genuine enthusiasm, each time you support their initiatives or address their concerns constructively, each time you publicly acknowledge their work.

- **Use collegial language.** Instead of saying "Let me help you get better at ____," try "I'd like to study ____ with you." This isn't just a quick word switch, it's the truth. If you're invested in improving the instruction in your school, you truly are interested in studying with and learning with this person.

- **Explain to the teachers how the coaching time will unfold.** Tell them about the scheduling, and reassure them that this is not evaluative. Clarify what your role and their role will be. If it seems like teachers are unsure or even resistant, you might want to explain that this is your way of keeping your own teaching self alive.

So, Just When Am I Supposed to Do This?

I know. You're busy. We're all busy. Being a principal has many, many facets to the job. The managerial and administrative parts of the work are over-whelming! How do you carve time into your busy life as a principal to coach teachers?

Our school year starts in September, so every August, I plan ahead for the next ten months, first for the time-bound work (the holidays, the school events, the district meetings, the faculty meetings, and the monthly drills and other activities that are required by law). Then, I plan for the work of instructional leadership (coaching, other professional development, and evaluations).

Once these times are in my calendar, I do not change them. Unless there's a major emergency, they stay. Of course, there are things that I can't possibly schedule this far in advance—meetings with parents, visits from other schools—but when I need to set these up, they go *around* what's already in there... including coaching!

Structuring This Work with Coaching Cycles

How much time do I allot for coaching? And what's the best time to do it? Over the years, I've found that the key to making coaching manageable is to schedule it in chunks called "coaching cycles." Figure 2.4 is a sample schedule for coaching cycles.

Of course, this schedule does *not* include every teacher in the school. That's because I am splitting the coaching load with our full-time literacy coach, Jaime. I make up the schedule for coaching cycles. Jaime and I usually switch, so teachers don't work with her more than two years in a row or with me for more than one year at a time. There are times of the year when multiple teachers are supported, and there are teachers who may be supported more than once. Schools with a large population may need to manipulate the length of each coaching cycle, making cycles shorter if you have more teachers you need to work with. Coaching isn't something people sign up for. The bottom line is that *everyone* is coached. It's not a sign of weakness--it's a sign of *strength*! Coaching is not for the teachers who struggle with something, or the new teachers: it's just something we *all* do.

FIGURE 2.4

SAMPLE SCHEDULE FOR COACHING CYCLES

Cycle	Teachers I'm Working With
1: September 9 to October 25	General Launch Helen G.
2: October 28 to December 20	Lori A. Danielle M. (coteachers)
3: January 2 to February 13	Chad P.
4: February 24 to April 25	All nontenured *(January hires)*
5: April 28 to June 25	Leah B. Sheila R. (coteachers)

Planning a Coaching Cycle

Before a new cycle begins, meet with each teacher you'll be coaching to plan out some goals for the work. This isn't just a formality: if a teacher asks to include something as a goal, it needs to be honored in the goals the two of you write together for this work. At the same time, you can use your own knowledge of the teacher's work to craft the work of the cycle.

Before your meeting with each teacher, use the notes you took in Figure 2.3 to make a menu of possible focuses you might feel comfortable with in your coaching. It's up to you to decide whether to share the list with teachers, but knowing what's on your own list can help you to consider options for what might be studied during the cycle. Of course, it's not an exhaustive list: other things can definitely be included in the coaching depending on what individual teachers need and are interested in. Figures 2.5, 2.6, and 2.7 give examples of coaching menus for literacy, math, and inquiry-based teaching.

As with any plan that embraces learning, coaching cycle plans are flexible and responsive to the learning. However, you can only be flexible when you have at least a rough idea of how you'll meet your goals. Just as teachers

FIGURE 2.5

SOME POSSIBLE CHOICES FOR OUR WORK TOGETHER IN LITERACY

Workshop Structures
Leveling libraries
Organizing writing centers
Arranging the room
Setting up conferring notes
Environments that create
    independence

Minilessons
Architecture of the minilesson
Deciding on a teaching point
Rigor in the minilessons
Using your own reading/writing
The art of demonstration
Alternative teaching methods

Conferring
Structure of the conference
Types of conferences
Rigor in the conference
Researching in conferring
Imagining strategy lessons
Complimenting
Using a learning progression to
    decide
Using your own reading/writing

Partner Work
Matching partners up
Listening in on conversation
Partner conferences
Teaching into metacognition
Management of partnerships

Share
Types of shares
Management of shares

Conversation
Read-aloud
Book clubs
A study of partnerships
Self-talk
Teaching kids to listen closely

Reading Assessment
Using the Teachers College
    assessment
Listening for accuracy
Miscue analysis
Fluency
Retelling: literal
Retelling: inferential
Using assessments to affect teaching

Reading levels
Studying reading levels up close
Guided reading

continues

SOME POSSIBLE CHOICES FOR OUR WORK TOGETHER IN LITERACY, *cont.*

Qualities of Good Writing
Content: choosing topics
Content: writing with focus
Content: writing what matters
Elaboration: choosing good detail
Elaboration: show, not tell
Structure: sorting information
Structure: writing with tension
Voice: mentor authors
Voice: tying it to convention
Convention: teaching into mechanics
Convention: manipulating it

Content Studies
Looking at specific units of study

Environments
Studying independence   .
Learning charts

Small-Group Work
Guided Reading: making a group
Guided Reading: choosing a text
Guided Reading: book introduction
Guided Reading: coaching into it
Guided Reading: following up
Strategy Lesson: choosing a group
Strategy Lesson: looking at structure
Strategy Lesson : following up
Other types of small-group work

Depths of Knowledge
Intro to Depths of Knowledge (DOK)
Using DOK in our minilessons
Using DOK in our conferring
Using DOK in our group work
Using DOK in our own reading/writing
Learning progressions
The art of inquiry

Management
Easy tips for transitions
Organization of materials
Cutting down time in our teaching
Teaching into independence

Read-Aloud
Building conversation through
    read-aloud
Tying reading aloud to minilessons
The nonfiction read-aloud
The whole-class conversation

Check Out My Teaching Moves
Conferences to strategy lessons
Pushing harder and pulling back

Pillars of Reading
Teaching into print work
Teaching into fluency
Teaching into literal comprehension
Teaching into inferential
    comprehension
Unifying components

FIGURE 2.6

SOME POSSIBLE CHOICES FOR OUR WORK TOGETHER IN MATH

Problem Solving
Setting up math projects/
    investigations
The role of talk in problem solving
The role of writing in problem solving
Differentiating problem solving
Fibonacci methods of problem solving
The role of pictures in problem solving

Developing Number Sense
Numeracy in operations
Using words/pictures to grow
    numeracy
Numeracy projects
Differentiating numeracy
Using base ten blocks to grow numeracy
Numeracy in geometry
Numeracy games
Using properties to build numeracy

STEM/Steam
Tying math to engineering
Math makerspaces
Math and science connections
The math of art

Computation
Using games to teach operations
Mnemonic devices
Alternative assessments in
    computation
Manipulatives that support
    computation
Differentiating computation
Technology to support computation

Methods of Differentiation
Small-group work revisited
Using manipulatives well
Scaffolding effectively
Using learning progressions

Assessment
Teaching students to self-assess
Assessment through projects
Assessment through writing
Assessment through talk
Item analysis
Using assessment to make plans

Content Studies: Multiplication
The conceptual side of multiplication
Using manipulatives to multiply
Using literature to help multiply
Multiplication projects

Management
Easy tips for transitions
Organization of materials
Cutting down time in our teaching
Teaching into independence

FIGURE 2.7

SOME POSSIBLE CHOICES FOR OUR WORK TOGETHER WITH TALK

Questioning
Using questions to set up inquiry
Essential questions in unit planning
Questioning in chapter books
Teaching partners to ask questions
Raising the levels of our questions

Partner Talk
Independence in partner talk
Using partners for accountability
Growing talk stamina for partners
Finding balance between partners
Partner talk in writing workshop

Talk as a Management Tool
Studying talk in our classroom
Talking out problems

Exploratory Talk
In reading
In writing
In math
In science
In social studies

create unit plans for an extended study of one topic, coaches and principals make cycle plans for their work with teachers. This work takes place during an initial meeting between you and the teacher. For example, when working with Kelsey, a relatively new teacher, we had goals that were content-related (unpacking the moves of entire units), structure-related (looking at how to confer when teaching reading), and classroom management-related. Tracy, a rather experienced teacher in our school, had wanted to study just how closely she listened to her students when conferring with them. She didn't need as much content or structural coaching. Focusing in on her listening helped her rethink her entire practice across the day.

When considering a teacher's individual goals, you're more able to determine the best structure for your coaching time. Sometimes, we work in a lab site, or a classroom during instruction of the area we are studying. This can be with one teacher or a whole group of them. Other times, we're in a study group, working outside the classroom to study student work or a professional text, although we might bring students in to try out small instructional moves. Other times, we might choose to have both a lab site component and a study group component. To keep the study group work from feeling too theoretical, we always incorporate real students into our work together.

Next, consider what coaching structure would be the most useful for this goal and this teacher: should all of the coaching take place in the lab site (the teacher's classroom), or should some of it also take place outside the classroom? Once you decide, use Figures 2.8 (lab site only) and 2.9 (lab sites and other study groups) to plan the work you'll do together over the coaching cycle.

Working Through the Coaching Cycle

There is a certain almost musical rhythm to the coaching cycle. As the teacher takes on more and more responsibility for concepts that have been introduced and practiced, the coach is able to introduce newer concepts. This way, as the cycle progresses, both the coach and the teacher stay very active in the learning process.

You can see this rhythm in the work I did with Ellen, a first-year fourth-grade teacher. At the beginning of our work together, Ellen and I agreed on three main focuses: the architecture of the minilesson, the basics of conferring, and using her own writing in her teaching. Over the six weeks we worked together, we practiced a gradual release of control. We began with minilessons. I started by modeling the entire minilesson. Then, week by week, Ellen took on more and more of the work, until finally, at the end of the cycle, she was teaching the entire minilesson, and I provided feedback.

We began our work by helping Ellen use her own writing with the class. First, Ellen modeled her own narrative writing. Then, a few weeks into the cycle, we layered in a second goal: working with a new type of writing, informational. Because we paid a great deal of attention to how Ellen used her own writing earlier in the cycle, she'd internalized it. Just as in our work with narratives, Ellen spent time writing informational pieces that she could use in her instruction. We'd modeled writing strategies for students to use with the teacher actually being a writer in front of them. This demonstration happened individually, in groups, and with the entire class. Ellen became confident in this area, and now knows that she can continue this on her own. Because she gets the basics of it, all we have to do is maintain that goal by trying it again.

FIGURE 2.8

PLANNING CYCLES OF COACHING AND STAFF DEVELOPMENT

Lab Site Work

Teacher(s)_____ Cycle Dates _____

Areas of Focus _____

Date	Coach Does	Teacher Does	Notes

FIGURE 2.9

PLANNING CYCLES OF COACHING AND STAFF DEVELOPMENT

Lab Site and Study Group Work

Teacher(s)_____ Cycle Dates _____

Areas of Focus _____

Date	Study Group Work	Lab Site Work (Coach)	Lab Site Work (Teacher)	Notes

The plan in Figure 2.10 illustrates how one goal is addressed with the coach's role and the teacher's role. The coach passes on more and more of the instruction to the teacher and shifts his or her goal toward giving feedback. While all this is going on with the goal of using one's own writing in instruction, other goals are being unpacked in similar ways (conferring, classroom management, content-specific knowledge).

FIGURE 2.10

THE GRADUAL RELEASE OF RESPONSIBILITY IN COACHING

	Coach Does	Teacher Does
Session 1	Coach models using his own writing in instruction (in lab site).	Teacher observes.
	Coach helps the teacher apply generating strategies so she can write her own piece (in study group).	Teacher writes a piece of her own.
Session 2	Coach prepares teacher to demonstrate explicitly using her own writing (in study group).	Teacher demonstrates using her own writing (not needing to explain the process).
	Coach explains to the class how the teacher will be using her own writing to illustrate what they will be doing themselves (in lab site).	
	Coach gives feedback to the teacher (in lab site).	
Session 3	Coach prepares teacher to use her own writing to teach a certain strategy both through demonstration and through direct instruction (in study group).	Teacher teaches using her own writing, demonstrating with it and giving direct instruction about her strategy (in lab site).
	Coach observes and gives feedback (in lab site).	
Session 4	Coach helps teacher brainstorm various strategies that can be taught through the teacher's writing (in study group).	Teacher brainstorms list of strategies that can be taught using her writing (in study group).
	Coach observes and gives feedback (in lab site).	Teacher uses writing in multiple conferences, each with their own teaching points (in lab site).

Coaching Methods and Structures

You've identified the need to coach. You've identified what you'll coach. You've carved out time to coach. You've named the people you'll coach and set goals for your work together. But what will you do when you're in the classroom?

Here are a few tried-and-true methods and structures of coaching—including a few developed at the Teachers College Reading and Writing Project—which principals, coaches, and staff developers have used over many years.

Study Group Coaching

When coaching teachers, there are two main settings we use: in the classroom (the lab site) and outside the classroom (study group). Each has its purpose. You would probably do most of your demonstration teaching in the lab site, because there, teachers can see the firsthand interaction between the students and the person who is delivering the methodology (sometimes the coach, sometimes the teachers). There are also a great many times where the study group setting can be more powerful: when looking at student work, when studying a professional resource like a text or video, or when engaging in longer or more discreet conversations that students are not meant to hear.

There are many valuable teaching methods we use during instruction such as demonstration, direct instruction, guided practice, and partner work. In the same way, there are also a variety of methods we use when *coaching* teachers. Here are a few methods of coaching that take place in the study group format of teacher coaching:

>**Reel to Real.** This is a great study group method for groups of teachers. Watch a professional video that can be viewed from various lenses. For example, when watching the video of a teacher conferring with one student, one lens might be to study the questions the teacher asks, another might be to watch how the body language of the student changes, and a third might be to notice how the teacher scaffolds or supports the student in trying out the new skill. Assign a lens of watching the video to each group of teachers, then have them discuss what they saw from that lens. You can then have each group share with the entire group. This approach works with professional texts also.

Graffiti Wall. A graffiti wall can be a great place to share new ideas and to spark important discussions. Place four or five large pieces of chart paper around the room with preprinted statements or questions related to a certain topic. Have teachers walk around and comment on each thought with a marker. After a few minutes, ask them to go around again and comment on other people's comments. If there are enough teachers and if there is enough time, ask teachers to gravitate around their favorite sheet and have a discussion. Then use the comments to springboard a whole-group discussion.

Coaching Bulletin Board. A coaching bulletin board helps to keep your coaching work on everyone's radar, and unlike some of the other ideas we've discussed here, it sets out some more universal thoughts that can be explored as an entire school. Find a bulletin board in a central location in the school. Choose a topic you'd like to explore with all your teachers and imagine the "chapters" or sections of the board that are a part of the topic. For example, a board on student independence might have sections on independence in classroom management, in instructional choices, and in materials. You might also have a section with a few professional articles. Then load the board with materials including handouts, pictures from classrooms in your school, or student work. Include a little blurb next to each item that annotates what the item is, and invite teachers to add things from their own classrooms.

Teaching Artifacts. To invite reflection at the end of a cycle of coaching, ask teachers to bring an artifact that is a metaphor for what they've learned during their work with you in the last few weeks. Often, the sillier the metaphor, the better!

Lab Site Coaching

The following methods are some that might be used in a lab site (classroom) setting with students. Just as we decide on a teaching method based on our audience and our content, we make similar choices when coaching teachers.

Before using any of these suggestions with teachers in the lab site, you might want to have a conversation with the students in the class so that they understand just what is about to happen. This conversation can look different at different age levels. With elementary students, you might say, "You know how learning something hard is better when you work on it with friends? Well, teaching is hard, and so sometimes, teachers get together and study what they do together. Isn't that cool? So when we're all in here, sometimes you'll hear us talking to you, and sometimes you'll hear us talking to each other, and that's OK. It's just how we learn."

With secondary students, you might say, "We're practicing what we do when we teach you so that we can always work on being the best teachers we can be. When you see us in here together, sometimes we'll just talk to each other or rewind something we just said. By sitting tight for a minute or so when that happens, you're helping us be the best teachers we can be for you."

Voicing Over. When watching the coach, the teacher sometimes won't know what to take away from the teaching, especially if a lesson is rich and the teaching moves are subtle. Using this method, the coach will teach, and while teaching, actually voice over himself, explaining to the teacher just what's going on, to help elaborate just how or why something was just done. By voicing over, we are shining the light right on what it is we hope they take away from what they've just seen.

Using Guide Sheets. When a coach is teaching in a classroom, teachers can use these scaffolded note-taking sheets to track what the coach is doing. Guide sheets (see Chapter 1 for an example) can be as simple as a checklist of very general terms that are checked off as the coach reaches that part of the teaching. In other cases, they might be more heavily scaffolded, acting almost as a script with the exact prompts a coach would use to bring attention to particular teaching moves. For example, part of the guide sheet might explicitly read, "Watch Tom as he names the teaching point with a specific skill and strategy in the minilesson. Now write that down, skill first, followed by the strategy." Like voicing over, guide sheets provide clarity for teachers who are watching very nuanced instruction in action.

Mirroring. Mirroring helps teachers learn the language of a certain methodology and gain deeper understanding of that methodology's structure. In mirroring, the coach starts by teaching a part of the lesson, and asks the teacher (or group of teachers) to simply repeat it. The coach can highlight certain phrases or other teaching moves for emphasis. If working with more than one teacher, participating teachers can work with students in small groups. For example, if the coach is working with four teachers, each will take one-fourth of the students and repeat the part just to them. After each part of the teaching, the coach moves on to the next part.

Freeze Frame. This method can be used when a teacher is working one-on-one with a student or with a small group. The teacher starts off the instruction while the coach takes notes. While this is going on, either the coach or the teacher can call a time-out to discuss what's going on, and reflect on any decisions that might need to be made before moving forward. The same can be done when the coach is teaching the students and the teacher is watching. The coach might freeze the instruction and turn to talk to the teacher to clarify what is going on or ask for feedback. The coach might also stop to ask a teacher to explain what she is thinking at a critical moment of the instruction.

Whispering In. This is done when the teacher is trying out what the coach has demonstrated. While the teacher is teaching, the coach literally whispers to the teacher, giving her some of the language to use when teaching. Just as in *Cyrano de Bergerac,* it's a situation where a more experienced or word-wise person offers assistance. Be careful not to jump into this too soon in your work with a teacher. This method requires some conversation and some relationship-building ahead of time, because it can throw a teacher off or even embarrass him or her in front of her students, or because some teachers might feel they are being corrected in front of their students. You might broach this topic by just saying, "I'd like to be able to ask you to rewind sometimes during the lesson. If you're OK with that, I'll give you a direction to try out on the spot. It might feel unusual at first, but it can really be helpful." Another way to build comfort in doing this is to ask the teacher to whisper to you when you're teaching her students.

Four Corners. This structure gives teachers an opportunity to try a lesson over and over again, honing it further with each repetition. Done in a lab site setting with multiple teachers, the teachers go in with lessons they have preplanned with a partner and teach their lesson in a small group in a corner of the classroom (hence the name!). During the first round, one teacher within the partnership teaches the lesson while the other observes. All the while, the coach goes around and whispers in, while also keeping time. The coach will announce the time so teachers can pace themselves appropriately. When the time is up, students will stand and go to another corner. While students are in transit, the teachers reflect on how to improve the lesson and switch roles. The understanding is that with each subsequent turn, the lesson will improve. Depending on the number of participants in the lab site, this can be with two or three or even six corners.

Reflecting on Your Work as a Coach

It's the end of the cycle. It's the end of this chapter. It's time to reflect. Amid all the myriad of responsibilities the principal faces, you've taken on coaching some of your teachers. In what ways was it worth sacrificing your precious time? How did you support teacher practice and student achievement? Our hope in this work is not that we carry the weight of student achievement in this coaching cycle. Our main job is not to teach a unit, but to use the unit to help the teacher grow so that he will move forward with better teaching habits than before because of your work together. Your time is an investment in this teacher and the students in her future. But how can you tell if this investment paid off?

First, there should be some reflection of your coaching work in student achievement. Student achievement doesn't always mean test scores. It could be in engagement, positive classroom environment, better work habits, self-confidence, a greater sense of independence, improved stamina, or more critical thinking. If you see evidence of improvements, you can note it in future observations (more on that in Chapter 4).

Second, you may see a more positive school culture as a result of this cycle. When you coach, you instill confidence in a teacher, not just in herself but also in you, as an instructional leader, guiding her and her colleagues toward a vision of what your school community views as student success. Sending a message that whatever you coached is something you believe in strongly helps your school community to see its principal as someone invested in learning alongside teachers and students in a collegial way. You'll know you've achieved this when the teachers come to you more and more with questions about instruction and learning, alongside those other, more typical questions about schedules and dealing with parents.

I opened this chapter with a quote by John Wooden, one of the greatest athletic coaches of the twentieth century. I'd like to close with a thought from Roland Barth, one of the greatest instructional leaders of that same century. Barth writes, "The most important feature of an educator is to provide the conditions under which people's learning curves go off the chart. Sometimes it is the other people's learning curves: those of students, teachers, parents, administrators. But at all times it is our own learning curve." (Barth 2007, 162) How did this cycle improve your own learning? How did it help shake up your thinking and shape who you are? How will it make you a stronger instructional leader at work tomorrow than you were today? How will you carry on this work?

Chapter 3

MANAGE YOUR SCHOOL WITH LEARNING IN MIND

*W*ill there be outdoor recess even though it's very cold? How will you deal with the angry parent on the phone, the broken intercom cutting off school-wide communication, the broken oven that means lunch will be delayed, the student-filled school bus that ran out of gas a mile down the road?* Being a principal involves a lot of day-to-day school management. At the same time, you also face decisions about your school community's long-term journey and how that community is helping students to learn.

Peg, an elementary school principal, has always been an inspiration for me in staying focused on student learning in my role as head learner. When I visited Peg's school as a staff developer, I was amazed by the sense of consistency in the school: everyone was on the same bus, headed in the same direction, and they trusted the principal. Teachers visited each other. The kids seemed happy. This wasn't the kind of false unity that comes with mandates or school-wide programs: the entire community seemed to share the same child-focused goals and value the same things. The students seemed to understand that no matter what class they were in, their school was a place where they were welcome and where they could learn. When I mentioned this to Peg, she explained that this was not always the case. When she came onboard, she felt that the school community was fractured. Classrooms felt isolated from one another. Teachers weren't actively working together. Norms varied across classrooms.

Kids learned to recalibrate their expectations, effort, and behavior depending where they were in the building and who was teaching them. It wasn't an environment for optimal learning.

So, how did Peg change this? Did she demand that every teacher teach the same things, the same way? Did she insist on school-wide behavioral norms? No. She started by giving her teachers and students opportunities to shine.

Peg cleared the first forty-five minutes of each Thursday morning for an all-school share. On a given Thursday, first graders might get up and share a science experiment in which they learned about animal adaptation, and third graders might share poetry they wrote. Not everyone shared every week, but, as the weeks moved on, more and more teachers and students *wanted* to participate in this celebration of learning. As teachers became more aware of what others were doing in the school, organic partnerships and coplanning sprang up. As children learned about what was happening in other parts of the building, they began to see the school as a whole community, not as a collection of individual classes. With Peg at the helm and offering support along the way, her school made a dramatic transformation.

Peg's story is a powerful reminder that sitting in the principal's office doesn't mean having to choose between being a learning leader and a manager. It means making management decisions guided by a vision of learning. Solutions like Peg's might seem magical. In fact, they're the result of thoughtful planning and careful implementation. This chapter's aim is to demystify the ways in which your management can support student learning.

In this chapter, we'll be looking at ways that you can design and use plans that are uniquely fitted to your school's needs. Just as reading and writing teachers follow the structure of research–decide–teach (Anderson 2000; Calkins 2001; Goldberg and Serravallo 2007) when conferring with students, school leaders can follow a research–decide–act structure when working with people in the school community to improve student learning. We begin our research by identifying what is going well in a segment of our school or the school as a whole and to learn where we can improve. Then, we decide which of those strengths to reinforce and what goals to set. Finally, we take action, reinforcing what is going well and developing plans for improving what still needs to become better.

Research the Issue

A few years ago, I was working with a large, urban elementary school. The principal was frustrated: the school was giving the teachers quality, intensive, in-person professional development. During the professional development sessions, teachers seemed receptive to the ideas presented. However, little changed in the school's classrooms. The teachers weren't putting what they'd learned to use.

It would be easy to make some pretty quick assumptions here about the teachers. An administrator might be tempted to conclude that the teachers had simply chosen to stick with what they already knew and ignore the new ideas. However, this principal was determined to consider the entire situation. As we looked at what was happening in individual teachers' classrooms, patterns started to emerge. Teachers on one team consistently mentioned some of the key terms they'd learned and even used structures like those taught in the professional development sessions, but the overall lessons weren't coherent or successful. Teachers on another team seemed to cling to only one isolated aspect of what they'd learned. Things became even clearer when the principal did more research to learn about how the vice principals had been supporting and assessing their teams. He found that, in the crush of other responsibilities and issues, the vice principals had offered little support for the instructional transitions. He also found that the evaluation methods that the vice principals were using had helped to form the classrooms that the principal was seeing: the vice principal who used a checklist to be sure that terms and structures were included gave rise to the disjointed classrooms of the first team. The vice principal who looked for a few favorite nuggets from the professional development was inadvertently encouraging teachers on the other team to focus on only those nuggets. Researching the issue helped the principal to see that it was the vice principals—not individual teachers—who needed his help in implementing the new instructional approach.

The research phase of our work gives us an opportunity to take a step back and truly get curious about what is happening in our school communities. Although some of the issues that we face may seem very easy to identify—a concern about test scores or staff morale, for example—we know that school issues typically have more causes and complexities than are immediately apparent.

Especially at this research stage, we must make an effort to listen to all of the messages we're taking in during our research, not only the messages that coincide with the causes or issues that were our initial focus.

This section suggests ways to research the issue you've identified. Some of the suggestions might, at first, sound like clearer fits for your issue than others. If you're trying to solve a truancy problem, for example, you'll likely be pouring over attendance data as part of your research. But don't discount the forms of research that might not be as obviously related. For example, you might decide to try visiting the classrooms of your truant students to see what it happening in the room.

Close-Read Your School's Documentation

In the last few years, close reading—the art of reading and rereading through a variety of lenses—has again become prominent in literacy instruction. As Lehman and Roberts (2014), Beers and Probst (2013) have shown, this kind of reading does not need to be a slog through a text. Instead, it can be a purposeful and meaningful inquiry that yields fresh insights in our research. With that same spirit of curiosity, you can close-read the documents related to your school to make new discoveries. Our schools are filled with documentation of teaching and learning that can set us on the path to improvement. Of course, we don't need to read everything to get a deeper understanding of every issue—if we're studying student behavior, we don't need to read the same artifacts we'd read if we were studying differentiated instruction or creativity or Norman Webb's Depths of Knowledge theory. See Figure 3.1 for a chart to help us consider (or remember) some of the help school documentation can provide.

Even when we focus on just a few types of documents, there's potential for information overload. What can we hope to remember, much less learn, by looking through report cards of a class, a grade, or even a school? We need to close-read with lenses to find patterns in the data. Filter questions like the following can help you to get started:

- What do I repeatedly see in the documentation? How often do I see it?
- Who is connected to this phenomenon? Who else might be involved in this phenomenon?
- Is there a certain time of year when this phenomenon occurs?
- Is there a certain subject related to this phenomenon?

DOCUMENTS TO CONSULT IN YOUR RESEARCH								
	Documents to Consult							
Area You're Researching	Attendance Records	Minutes from Faculty Meetings	Minutes from Professional Development Sessions	Minutes from PTA Meetings	Report Cards	Student Writing	Teacher Observations	Test Scores
Assessment					X	X		X
Consistency across classrooms/curriculum alignment						X	X	X
Differentiated instruction					X	X	X	X
Fund-raising				X				
Instruction in particular subject areas					X	X	X	X
Parent relations				X				
Professional development			X			X	X	X
School climate		X	X	X				
Special education					X	X	X	
Staff morale	X	X						
Student achievement	X				X	X		X
Truancy	X							

FIGURE 3.1

Then, once we've identified patterns, we can consider what those patterns mean. Do the phenomena you've identified seem to be isolated issues or part of a trend? What larger issue(s) in the school might it point to? What does this make us know or wonder about the instruction that goes on in our school? Many times, instruction is at the heart of what's best and worst about our schools. If we consider an issue from an instructional stance, we'll likely get to the root of it.

Read the Halls

You can continue your research by going for a walk around the hallways of your school—it will help you to pick up on school-wide trends and to get a feel for what is going on in particular grade levels, teams, or classrooms. The halls of a school show us what the school community values. For example, many school hallways are filled with student work. But what does the artwork reveal about the teaching behind it? The questions in Figure 3.2 can help us to consider what we see in the hallways at our school.

HOW TO USE THE TOOLS IN THIS CHAPTER

As you use the question lists and checklists in this chapter, be mindful of how you're employing these tools with the faculty and students in your school. I've designed them to be user-friendly and quick to complete. Although it might be tempting to simply carry around a clipboard with a stack of tools, continuously making notes, be wary of "checklisting" people's work, which can feel adversarial. Don't let the tools get in the way of real interactions with others.

Also, although some of these tools might be excellent fits for what you need right now, feel free to consider them as models—editing, revising, and using them as springboards for creating your own tools. Consider your own needs, not only the directions that the existing tools take.

You might wonder which classrooms you should visit. The short answer: visit them all. You want to have a presence in the entire school. Even a quick in-and-out will give you time to ask a child what they're learning.

Finally, keep in mind that these tools are for looking for trends, not for evaluating individual teachers. As Andy Hargreaves and Michael Fullan (2012) point out, the best model for school improvement is one in which we develop teachers' skills *as a group*.

FIGURE 3.2

READING THE HALLS: QUESTIONS TO CONSIDER

Teacher/Class: _____ Date: _____ Grade: _____

1. **What teaching and learning went into creating this artifact?** *Consider:*
   - How long did this work take students? Teachers?
   - How complex is this work? In what ways does it show students' higher-order thinking?
   - Is this product the result of skills that can be used again and again?
   - Are kids synthesizing and applying skills, or simply copying a model?

2. **How much of this is the teacher and how much the student?** *Consider:*
   - What was obviously controlled by the teacher? By the student?
   - How much significant choice were students given?
   - Do you get the sense that students are genuinely proud of the work?
   - Are kids taking risks in their work?

3. **How consistent is the work throughout the school?** *Consider:*
   - Do hallway artifacts suggest similar practices throughout the school?
   - Does it seem that you can see the influence of one teacher or grade level more clearly than others?

4. **What values does this work show?** *Consider:*
   - What values do the artifacts seem to promote: Product or process? Conformity or innovation? Approximation or perfection? Remediation or celebration?
   - What does the work show as strengths in the school?

5. **What next steps might these observations suggest?** *Consider:*
   - Is there evidence of the work teachers have undertaken recently?
   - What evidence is there of initiatives supported through staff development or directives?
   - What would make sense to work on with our teachers based on what you're seeing?

6. **What else do you notice?**

Circle any items on this list that require follow-up or that inform your inquiry. What will you research or do next?

Visit Classrooms

Classroom visits are telling forms of research, whether we are interested in a very specific issue (relating to a particular grade, subject, or classroom) or an issue that touches the entire school. When we sit in on a meeting in which teachers talk about practice, we learn a lot about theory; but we know that when we visit teachers and learners in their natural habitat, we get a more authentic picture of what is going on. As visitors in classrooms, we see not only the methods of instruction but also the silent types of communication, unarticulated but nevertheless visible cues to learning, power, values, activity, and passivity (body language, room arrangement, charts and materials, silence), not to mention the social dynamics (the leaders and the followers; attitudes toward celebration, pride, fear, risk, tolerance, acceptance, isolation).

This is a tremendous amount of information to take in. For the visits that we make as part of our research, we can use an agenda or a lens to help us identify the strengths and needs of our school, keeping in mind that our focus is on our research at this point, not on evaluating individual teachers. Our goal in all of this work is to find a plan that will improve the *entire* school. Figures 3.3–3.9 document some lenses through which we can observe classrooms.

By analyzing who owns the talk in the classroom (the teacher, the students, or both) and what role the talk plays (managerial and procedural, communicating fact and recall, or developing ideas), we can better see how learning happens in the class.

Watch Interactions

Paying attention to the way that the people in the school interact can be another form of research, helping us to identify issues in the school. Personally, when I've seen disrespect in schools—among students, between students and teachers, and among teachers—it's been nearly impossible to advance new initiatives. When we, as principals, chalk this kind of behavior up to being part of others' natures and don't address it directly, we're hampering our school's potential.

In this chapter, we've been looking at ways to research issues in our schools so that we can find solutions that will advance student learning. So, why should we look at interpersonal interactions in school? Isn't social-emotional learning separate from academics? Actually, no. Citing a 2011 meta-analysis by Durlak

Scholars from Eleanor Duckworth (1991) to Elizabeth A. City (City et al. 2014) have taught us about the importance of talk and listening in the process of learning. For people to learn, they have to process what they are learning, to grow ideas of their own. Talking helps them to do that. Insisting that kids stay quiet turns their problem-solving button off.

FIGURE 3.3

CLASSROOM VISITS:
EAVESDROPPING ON TALK IN A CLASSROOM

Teacher/Class: _____ Date: _____ Grade: _____

When using this tool, visit the classroom long enough to see both the teacher and the students talking. Visit during different points in the day to see if findings are consistent.

Who owns the talk?

The teacher does most of the talking.	Yes	No
The students do most of the talking.	Yes	No
The teachers and the students do an equal share of the talking.	Yes	No

What kinds of questions does the teacher ask?

The teacher asks many low-level, closed-ended questions.	Yes	No
The teacher asks many high-level, open-ended questions.	Yes	No
The teacher asks questions to which more than one answer might be correct.	Yes	No

What is the nature of the teacher talk in the room?

The teacher gives mainly directional or correctional cues.	Yes	No
The teacher models strategies being taught.	Yes	No
The teacher names strategies being taught.	Yes	No

What is the nature of partner talk in the room?

Partners have lots of time to talk.	Yes	No
Partners engage in cumulative conversation.	Yes	No
Partners engage in metacognitive conversation.	Yes	No

What else do you notice?

Consider your notes above, keeping in mind that a *yes* is not always a positive and a *no* is not always a negative. How does conversation in this classroom help facilitate learning?

Circle any items on this list that require follow-up or that inform your inquiry. What will you research or do next?

> *When we're considering issues such as student performance, student autonomy, and classroom instruction, the environment may hold some clues for us. In our best classrooms, the walls of the room help teach as well, allowing students to be independent through reminders of what has been taught. This sheet helps us gauge the helpfulness of the charts in student learning.*

FIGURE 3.4

CLASSROOM VISITS: LOOKING AT LEARNING CHARTS

Teacher/Class: _____ Date: _____ Grade: _____

Are the charts user-friendly?

The charts allow kids to remember strategies that were taught.	Yes	No
The charts are neat and legible.	Yes	No
The charts are written in terms that kids can understand.	Yes	No

Are the charts displayed so that kids can use them easily?

The charts are organized into clusters according to subject.	Yes	No
The charts are located at a comfortable eye level.	Yes	No

Do the charts change and grow with the kids?

There are more teacher-/student-created charts than commercial charts.	Yes	No
The current charts reflect current units of study.	Yes	No

Is there a variety to the kinds of charts in the room?

There are charts that are strategy oriented.	Yes	No
There are charts that are management oriented.	Yes	No
There are charts that are conversation oriented.	Yes	No

The *yes* responses above might indicate a student-focused classroom. How do the charts in this classroom help to facilitate learning?

Circle any items on this list that require follow-up or that inform your inquiry. What will you research or do next?

Environments where kids feel comfortable taking risks and stretching outside their comfort zone are often marked by a culture of celebration: when we celebrate compliments in class, celebrate student work by making it a model for others, or celebrate a student's academic growth with the class, the class naturally becomes more student centered. Learning experiences automatically have a much more authentic context, making them more real. Although this sheet looks at rooms through the lens of celebration, you might consider it a study of student centeredness.

FIGURE 3.5

CLASSROOM VISITS: A CULTURE OF CELEBRATION

Teacher/Class: _____ Date: _____ Grade: _____

Bulletin Boards

The bulletin boards reflect students' best work.	Yes	No
The bulletin boards are more than 50 percent student designed.	Yes	No

Conversation

Students feel free to talk and take risks in conversation.	Yes	No
The teacher asks questions that have many right answers.	Yes	No

Environment

Students had a hand in designing aspects of the room.	Yes	No
The language of management is positively oriented.	Yes	No

Writing

Students' published pieces are displayed somewhere in the room.	Yes	No
When asked to share their writing with you, students do so with little or no hesitation.	Yes	No

What else do you notice?

The *yes* responses above might indicate a student-focused classroom. Circle any items on this list that require follow-up or that inform your inquiry. What will you research or do next?

In the interest of promoting student innovation and engagement, we want to encourage environments that foster high levels of student independence. Just as we, as teachers, appreciate school environments in which we can be independent and innovative in our work, students who have voice and choice are more likely to be engaged than simply compliant. In a school of teacher-controlled classrooms, there's too much energy spent on control. The adults in the school may not be able to hear the kids' needs as clearly because they're busy managing them.

FIGURE 3.6

CLASSROOM VISITS: LOOKING AT INDEPENDENCE AND CONTROL

Teacher/Class: _____ Date: _____ Grade: _____

	Teacher Control →		Neutral →		Student Independence
Classroom Management					
The students have a role in the creation/revision of rules and procedures.	1	2	3	4	5
The students have jobs which they do without much prompting.	1	2	3	4	5
Conversation					
The students are free to consult a partner when needed without permission.	1	2	3	4	5
The students are free to ask the teacher a question when confused.	1	2	3	4	5
The room is physically arranged to encourage collaboration all the time.	1	2	3	4	5
Choices About Reading					
The students are allowed to choose their own books to read.	1	2	3	4	5
The students are allowed to respond to their reading in any way.	1	2	3	4	5
The students grow their own ideas in their books.	1	2	3	4	5
Choices About Writing					
The classroom has many charts that remind students of what they've learned.	1	2	3	4	5
The classroom has a word wall to help them spell difficult words.	1	2	3	4	5
The students have easy access to clearly labeled materials.	1	2	3	4	5

What else do you notice?

Ideally, we should see a trend of student independence in our schools. Circle any items on this list that require follow-up or that inform your inquiry. What will you research or do next?

If you're researching an issue that relates directly to academics, you may want to examine the continuity of instruction in a particular subject across grades or across classrooms within a grade: the third-grade teacher can't stand on the shoulders of the second- or first-grade teachers if their instruction isn't aligned. This chart shows how you might examine the continuity of balanced literacy instruction, but you can also use the chart as a model for examining other instructional areas, swapping out the criteria in the top row with criteria for the chosen subject.

FIGURE 3.7

RESEARCHING OUR SCHOOLS: CONSISTENCY IN LITERACY INSTRUCTION ACROSS CLASSES OR GRADES

Date: _____

If you're considering continuity across a single grade level, consider every teacher in that grade level. If you're considering continuity across grade levels, consider a teacher whose practices are representative of their entire grade from each grade level.

Teacher	Units	Environment	Leveled Library	Published Work	Charts
	In what ways do the units build on each other from year to year?	Describe the physical arrangement of the room. What does it show?	What are the levels of the books? What special sections are there to the library?	Is there published work displayed? What can you tell from it?	Do the charts indicate current units? Were they made with students?

What else do you notice?

What generalizations can be made about this school?

FIGURE 3.8

CLASSROOM VISITS: QUESTIONS TO CONSIDER
AFTER THE VISIT

Teacher/Class: _____ Date: _____ Grade: _____

1. **What is the most interesting or surprising piece of information you gleaned during this visit?** *Consider:*
   - How does this visit compare with your expectations?

2. **Upon repeated visits, perhaps at different times of the day, do your observations change?** *Consider:*
   - What factors might account for different observed behaviors? A different subject?

3. **What trends to you see beyond this classroom?** *Consider:*
   - Are there trends based on grade levels, subject areas, or years of experience?

4. **What else do you notice?**

Circle any items on this list that require follow-up or that inform your inquiry. What will you research or do next?

FIGURE 3.9

CLASSROOM VISITS: LOOKING AT RELATIONSHIPS AND INTERACTIONS

Location: _____ Date: _____ Grade: _____

	Always	→	**Never**

Structured, Instructional Time

Everyone is respectful of the speaker.	1	2	3	4	5
Divergent answers are considered.	1	2	3	4	5
Classroom rules are followed so learning can happen.	1	2	3	4	5

Unstructured, Instructional Time

Students listen to one another's ideas.	1	2	3	4	5
Teachers listen to students' ideas.	1	2	3	4	5
Students listen to teachers' ideas.	1	2	3	4	5

Unstructured, Noninstructional Time

Adults speak to one another respectfully.	1	2	3	4	5
Students speak to one another respectfully.	1	2	3	4	5
Adults and students speak to one another respectfully.	1	2	3	4	5
School rules are generally followed.	1	2	3	4	5

et al., Stephanie Harvey and Harvey Daniels (2015, xiii) explain that "kids who are directly taught how to be peaceful, friendly, and supportive in the classroom not only avoided much conflict, but also saw 11 percent gains in course grades and standardized test scores." How kids are feeling and acting at school affects their learning.

Get Second (or Third or Fourth) Opinions

A few years ago, a friend and fellow principal was having a frustrating problem: he knew that something wasn't working in one of the classrooms in his school, but he couldn't quite put his finger on what the issue was. He visited the classroom, spoke with the teacher, observed the kids—but he couldn't pinpoint what was making the atmosphere in the room unfriendly. So, he asked a colleague from another school to sit in on the classroom. A few minutes later, to the principal's surprise, the colleague returned and simply said that the class felt, to him, too teacher-centered. He gave a few examples and reasons. My friend was stunned—how had he missed this?

So far, we've discussed research that you can do on your own. That's a great way to get started, but it's only a start. To get a true picture of the issues in your school, you need to invite others into the conversation as well. In my friend's situation, an outside expert was able to see the heart of the issue clearly because he was looking with fresh eyes. Stakeholders—the teachers, the students, the parents—can also help us take the learning pulse of the community. Conversations with stakeholders help us to plan the next steps on how our school can grow, but they also help the plans to be more successful: when ideas are developed communally, everyone is invested because they've had a role in their formation.

We wouldn't be in this job if we didn't have strong leadership skills already, but this kind of work—inviting others to share ideas and even criticisms—can be particularly delicate. There is no one right way to involve others in our research, but the following guidelines have been a help to me in my work.

> **Identify the people you'd like to talk with.** When you're exploring ideas, it can feel safest to reach out to the people who are most obviously involved with the issue and the people you know best. However, you might also find valuable perspectives beyond this circle. Consider:

- Who is the best authority on the issue you're exploring?
- Who's available?
- Who has a long connection with your school or district?
- Who brings a fresh perspective to your school or district?
- Who has strengths that could help you with this issue?
- Who has experience or beliefs that make them passionate about this issue?
- Who can give you a clear idea of a teacher's perspective on this issue? A coach's? A parent's? A student's?

It's possible that some—or all—of the people you talk to will have a bias of some kind. An individual's bias might make him answer your questions with great passion, or it might keep him from seeing beyond their own experiences. Weigh people's histories and passions as you consider their input.

Speak with and listen to others with genuine curiosity and interest. Just as we don't try to get a clear picture of students' understandings and realities by asking a few yes-or-no questions, we need to engage people with open-ended questions that show that we value their thinking. Wait time and follow-up questions are as valuable in speaking with adults as they are when we're in the classroom working with students.

Put others at ease. Even when we approach this work with an open mind and a generous heart, there's a chance that faculty and staff may wonder about our intentions. Sadly, the work that goes on in schools has been so maligned in recent years that educators have become wary of situations that may feel like surreptitious evaluations or the leading edge of some sort of disruptive attempt at reform. Avoiding inflammatory language (words like *crisis, forever, always, never, terrible, disaster*) and keeping the conversations as casual as possible are good ways to begin. Using language that creates a sense of community (using *we* and *us* instead of *I, me,* and *you*) and sitting side by side with teachers in their classroom can subtly let teachers know that you are not acting as an authoritarian in this work. Framing the conversation from the perspective of student achievement can help to break the ice when a topic is uncomfortable: no matter one's beliefs regarding teaching and learning, everyone wants students to be successful.

Finally, ending the conversation by summing up the main points discussed and thanking the person for her help and time communicates respect and collegiality.

Take notes in the most useful way possible. Sometimes taking notes in front of people makes them feel what they're saying is important and they'll share even more insights. However, taking copious notes can also make people nervous, inhibiting their willingness to share. Consider what's right for the situation. If it doesn't seem helpful to take notes during the conversation, find time to write things down afterward.

Invite dissent. When we keep in mind that our work at this stage is to listen and learn, everyone—even (or especially) people with whom we rarely see eye to eye—can help us to learn. Resist the temptation to try to promote a particular idea at this point. If you find that you must disagree with someone in this conversation, follow up on the point with *because* and state your opinion, always from the stance of student achievement. Additionally, if you need to cite research, naming particular sources helps people to know that you're talking about specific, real data, not just a general interpretation of research. Use these strategies sparingly: winning an argument here will not help you with your research, and it may put the people you're arguing with on the defensive.

Define, Then Refine, the Plan

Now that you've done your research, it's time to make a plan. But, with so much information—and possibly some conflicting viewpoints—where do you begin?

The best news about thorough research—as well as the worst—is that we can expect anything. Issues we might not have considered may have come to light; we may have gone looking for research about the learning climate and discovered the problematic role of a particular program in our school community. Alternatively, you might have been forming a plan during the research stage of your work, and it may be helpful to look at it critically before implementing it. Either way, the following questions might help you to find a pattern in the data you've collected or to carefully consider a plan you're already forming.

- **What's the source of this information?** We may be particularly good at plumbing a particular source—examining physical layouts, listening to students talk, reading student writing, reading through lesson plans or past observations—and therefore better at acquiring information that way. Naming the source also helps us see whether we're taking more information from quantifiable sources (test scores, for example) or more subjective ones (our personal thoughts and opinions). The more sources we are able to use, the deeper insight we're able to gain.

- **What's significant or surprising?** We may have discovered lots of interesting facts and observations from each source, but not everything we notice is going to change the world. We need to name the information that is something we have not noticed before or that might have widespread effects. In answering this question especially, be cautious of overgeneralizations and aware that a single data point might just be a snapshot caught on a bad day.

- **How do the findings affect instruction in the school?** Keeping a clear focus on our roles as instructional leaders, not merely building managers, can help us to discriminate between data that are central to our goals and data that are really only noise.

- **What does this make me consider?** These notes might be questions or even possible solutions.

Involve Others

Once we've zeroed in on the most revealing information, it's time to confer with a trusted colleague or a stakeholder. Being a leader doesn't mean going it alone. When we lean on the strength of the relationships described in Chapter 1, we increase the amount of personal investment and interest our stakeholders have. We're also more likely to find a solution that works well for everyone involved.

A variety of school and district shareholders have a clear and direct interest in a school's success: teachers, staff, parents, and district-level staff.

But many people beyond that circle can also provide input and help, including community members, consultants, and a group often overlooked: other principals, in nearby districts and across the country, who may have experience we can learn from.

Start with the issue you're facing and then consider who might be a good person to turn to for support (see Figure 3.10).

FIGURE 3.10

GATHERING SUPPORT FOR ISSUES WE FACE		
If we need support with . . .	**We might need someone who . . .**	**Like . . .**
A curriculum issue related to a specific subject	Loves teaching that subject Has learned a lot about that subject	
A learning climate issue	Has dealt with difficult climate issues Is good at making peace Has been a principal for a long time	
Organization and management	Is the leader of a similar-sized school Is organized	
A historical school issue	Has a long history with the school or Knows the school from an outsider's perspective	
Creating a least restrictive environment for students with special needs	Supervises special education and has worked with many structures of special education Inherently understands differentiation Is a good scheduler	

We can replace the issues in Figure 3.10 with anything relevant to our situation. The most important facet of figuring out who can help us work on the solution we need is knowing stakeholders, colleagues, teachers, parents, community members, and their strengths and talents.

Unlike the information-gathering sessions you held earlier, the conversations you'll have with these people will be work sessions, in which you're actively trying out ideas together. Because of your position as principal, it's possible that some faculty or staff members may need encouragement to share ideas, particularly if they're dramatically different ideas. If you find the conversation getting stuck, stretching phrases like these can help draw out more ideas:

- That must mean. . . .
- That reminds me of. . . .
- This is important because. . . .
- Could that be because. . . ?
- So what you're saying is. . . .
- That's so surprising because. . . .

Use Your Administrative Capital

Although our work as instructional leaders emphasizes the work we do to help children to learn, the administrative responsibilities that come with the job of being a principal need not be at odds with our goals for instruction. Instead, we can leverage our administrative decisions to support the solutions we put into action to improve instruction.

When studying to be a principal, we learned about ways to use management decisions to solve any type of problem. This accepted management wisdom holds that there are four foundational resources for dealing with an organization-wide problem, whether the organization is a school, a family, or an international corporation: money, personnel, time, and space. One way to force our inner manager to think creatively is to consider each of these resources a lens through which to look for possible solutions. *How could I address this problem with money? With personnel? With time? With space?* Some solutions involve more than one category, and that's OK: our purpose is to generate ideas, not classify them.

Our inner leader also has an important role here: for every suggestion our manager makes, our inner leader asks how this will make kids' learning better. If it doesn't make learning better, we don't add it to the list.

At this stage, it's OK to consider outrageous responses as long as they focus on kids' learning. Sometimes the crazier the response, the more successful it will be.

How Can Money Help?

All of us, I'm sure, have had that daydream of what we could do with our schools if we only had better funding. However, even the best-funded schools can face difficulties. Money can help us to attain what we need—consultants, professional books, technology, personnel, substitutes to give teachers time to plan and learn, improved facilities—but we only know what we need and how to use it effectively when we have a clear educational vision.

It might feel easy to simply skip this section and conclude that there isn't any money to be had in your district. However, we shouldn't rule out money just because something we're imagining isn't already a line item in our budget. Even in these difficult financial times, we can find ways to acquire the funds necessary to execute our vision. If we have access to a viable parent organization or educational foundation, we're lucky. If these organizations share our educational vision, even better! However, learning-based fund-raisers are also key. In our school, we've raised money by partnering with a local bookstore for a "read-in" with kids and parents, developing programs in which students find adult sponsors who donate money as the children meet goals in school (a quarter for each new math fact or a dollar for every pound of recyclables they gather for a unit on the environment), and even hosting a museum night at school in which parents and families pay an admission fee to see student artwork and writing and to hear students perform.

How Can People Help?

When we let stakeholders in our school help us, we not only solve the problem but also strengthen the community. Everyone, students and adults alike, is more committed to a plan when that plan values them as individuals. Following are a few possibilities:

- A teacher or staff member with a special academic talent (writing, knowledge in a specific subject, mechanical drawing)
- A teacher or staff member with a special personal talent (artistic, organizational, social)

- A parent with specialized training (lawyer, chef, management consultant, journalist)
- Local businesses willing to donate their services (printing, construction, gardening, catering)
- Students with special talents
- Colleagues in a neighboring school or district

The people you rely on at this stage will become the core of the leadership team that helps you to implement your improvement plan.

How Can a Better Use of Time Help?

Especially when we are new to a school, we may not feel that we are able to use finances or direct personnel in the way we'd like. We may not have hired the teachers. We may not have the freedom to spend money the way we want to. However, we do control the way we spend our time, and we can make changes to the school's master schedule. Managing time can call to mind images of a taskmaster with a stopwatch, but the thoughtful use of time can help us to emphasize the things we value. For example, in our school, we've adjusted the way we schedule and use time to maximize in-class support by clustering students with similar needs in the same class, which means that support teachers don't have to teach the same lesson in multiple classes. We've also used time to promote staff development by dealing with housekeeping items via email and reserving faculty meeting time for teacher discussion groups to solve school issues and for learning time in which an expert presents new ideas.

How Can the School's Physical Space Help?

Just as we can allocate time to focus on what we value, we can reimagine the physical spaces in the school to focus on enhancing the learning taking place there. A prominent, well-maintained bulletin board devoted to teacher learning or a meeting space stocked with professional development materials can not only recognize and give new life to good practices but also spur new learning. Setting up book nooks around the school where children can spend extra time reading as a reward gives students extra time to practice the act of reading and associate it with reward, not work.

How Might These Four Factors Come Together in a Complete Plan?

A few years ago, I worked with my team to address improving writing instruction in our school. Figure 3.11 shows some of the ideas that we decided to implement. Creating a table like the one in Figure 3.11 helps us brainstorm actions we can put into place right away that will have immediate results, as well as long-term ones that will play out over months or years.

As you can see, some of the ideas require more work than others, and some have more long-term effects than immediate effects. However, they are all working toward the same purpose.

FIGURE 3.11

FOUR RESOURCES MODEL FOR FINDING SOLUTIONS

Financial Resources	Human Resources	Temporal Resources	Spatial Resources
Hire an outside staff developer from a professional development organization to conduct regular visits and work with the teachers on literacy instruction. Purchase professional texts on literacy instruction.	Create teacher-led study groups that meet before or after school to dig deep into literacy instruction. Hire a literacy coach to support professional learning around reading and writing instruction.	Insert time into teachers' weekly schedule for common planning and professional development. Implement regular interclassroom or interschool visits during which teachers study literacy.	Create a literacy curriculum center where teachers can gather and analyze resources. Create bulletin boards on which teachers share lesson plans, charts, and other resources.

Delegating Responsibilities and Setting Goals

If I had tried to implement all of these ideas on my own, it would have been disastrous. These ideas address the issue from so many angles that I would never have been able to manage them all, much less manage them well. More important than the managerial piece of this, however, is the sense of community and ownership that the leadership team brought to this work. Delegating responsibilities to this team empowered faculty to develop their own skills.

Our role at this stage is not to spearhead every initiative but to support the initiators we designate. For example, if we decide that the literacy coach will help teachers lead writing conferences, we have to provide support, giving the coach time to plan, announcing the policy as a school-wide initiative, and scheduling time in which the coach can work with teachers individually or in teams.

One way to help others see their progress is to set goals that lay out the timeline of the work's success, not simply a single end goal. When the first success happens early in the process, momentum builds exponentially.

As you map out the goals for each action, consider this framework:

- **The initiator.** Who will facilitate the team's first actions? How will you and others support him?

- **The audience.** Who will demonstrate the greatest change because of the action?

- **Approximate time frame.** How much time has been allotted for the initial success? (The first success needs to come quickly and to be easily measurable. If it doesn't, the goal needs to be modified.)

- **Action.** What will the audience do to experience success?

- **Measurement.** How will all the stakeholders recognize that they have achieved success?

- **Support.** How will we support success for our key initiator and the audience? What money, personnel, time, and space will we allocate?

- **Celebration.** How will we acknowledge (and thus reinforce) success? How will the celebration segue into the next goal?

- **Gradual release of control.** How will the key audience own the initial success and work with it independently, so that the key initiator can introduce the next level of the goal? If the members of the learning community can carry on what they've learned without us, our vision will be our legacy. This step is critical in both the short and long term.

You'll notice that the final stages of these guidelines place more responsibility on the team and less on you. Additionally, the final stages anticipate a next action, next focus, or next issue. The work is never done. By focusing on our long-term vision, we avoid becoming *administrators*, or managers who carry out *other people's* visions. By staying in touch with the on-the-ground realities of our schools and by supporting our leadership teams, we avoid becoming *dreamers*, or managers who are never really able to make their ideas work. Instead, we are *leaders,* in the truest sense of the word—establishing a vision (often a shared one) whose stages we guide (often with others) from idea to reality.

Putting the Plan into Action

Those of us who have been learning leaders for a long time have seen countless initiatives come and go. A teacher relative asked me at a family gathering last September, "What new initiative is your district doing this year?" She expected a new buzz word that would be forgotten a year later. It made me see that yes, some districts go through the motions of a new initiative every year just to say they have a new initiative. But there are Septembers in which we don't tout a new initiative but deepen an ongoing one. I replied, "We don't have *a* new initiative this year. We're continuing to grow in the work of the last few years." After a moment of confusion, she smiled and said how satisfying it must be to stick with something big for the long haul.

Hopping from initiative to initiative every year is symptomatic of a lack of vision, which can be read as confusion, jadedness, apathy, even hostility. When we unveil something new to work on together, we must walk lightly. Teachers are at their best when they can innovate. We want to make them feel they have a part in the creation of the new work. If something new is presented top-down, the license to innovate is revoked. Therefore we need to:

- Find a connection to something teachers are already doing. This will make the new work seem more relevant, familiar, comfortable, and attainable.

- Casually mention the research, formal or anecdotal, that supports what we are about to undertake together.

- Explicitly name the ways in which they will be supported in this new endeavor.

- Be flexible. Although there are often very linear steps we take in making change, the really important work of the classroom (or any important work) is three-dimensional and messy. We need to be prepared for that.

Evaluating Progress

Once we have released control, we have to put on our other hat. Till now, we've been facilitators, supporters, cheerleaders, timekeepers. Now, to sustain what's been achieved, we have to expect it and evaluate it, conducting regular observations of teachers as they carry out the initiative and give them feedback. Chapter 4 delves into what this entails.

We must also evaluate ourselves as facilitators. Here are some questions to help us figure out how we're doing:

- Whose work have I made easier through my support? How has that had an impact on student achievement?
- Are my expectations of others and myself realistic yet rigorous?
- Am I realistic with the amount of time I expect something to take? Are there parts of my expectation that should take longer? Not as long?
- Are we really measuring what we say we're measuring?
- Am I keeping my eyes on the long-term goal, or am I focusing too hard on the immediate goal?
- How am I motivating others throughout this process?
- In what ways am I communicating most effectively? Which stakeholders am I not paying enough attention to?

Managerial Moves That Support Learning: A Case Study for Improving Reading Achievement

In this chapter, we've considered options for keeping learning at the forefront when making managerial decisions about the school. Now, let's take a look at what researching an issue, making a plan, and implementing the plan look like in the real world, with all of the moving parts and variables that our jobs entail.

Like many principals living in this testing age, I was curious about the reading levels of my students. There is a strong correlation between students' independent reading levels and their success on standardized tests in reading (Allington 2001). How were my students doing?

Researching the Issue

My concern heightened when I reviewed the reading levels of my students. I found that many more were reading below grade level than I had thought. In fact, some students who seemed bright in many other ways were struggling with their reading. I worried about this, not just because of the tests that were looming but because the gaps that establish themselves in elementary school increase as students became older. We needed to do everything we could to close those gaps.

After reviewing teachers' plan books, I noticed that most teachers were teaching reading for a forty-minute period to stick with the overall forty-minute block schedule of the day. When I observed classes, I saw that within those precious forty minutes, minilessons often went longer than ten minutes, sometimes leaving students with as little as fifteen minutes a day to read! There are strong bodies of evidence supporting a correlation between the amount of time students spend reading texts that they can read with independence and their success on reading tests. For example, a study by Richard Allington (2001) correlates low achievement with dramatically fewer words read: children who achieved in the 10th percentile read only about 51,000 words each year, and those who achieved at the 90th percentile read about 2,357,000 words per year. Our students needed more time to read.

A walk through the hallways suggested that although we were adept at celebrating writing by posting published pieces, there were very few classrooms that celebrated *reading* in such a way. In fact, when reading the halls, I only found two reading bulletin boards: one was celebrating the picture book series of an author who was just about to visit the school, and one was a very teacher-directed bulletin board with some prompted writing about what students liked to read.

During the same walk in the hallway, I asked random students who were passing by what they thought about reading. One student just shrugged her shoulders. Another told me proudly, "I'm a level M." A few of the older students from various classrooms said that they liked reading, and they didn't seem to have enough time to read. Some others said their teachers were reading aloud some funny books. Beyond the question of level (with which that student at level M seemed to be *over* identifying), students didn't seem to think they had much control over their reading lives.

Classroom visits during reading time yielded some interesting information. When listening in on the talk during reading workshop, I noticed that some teachers were giving students only a few minutes of partner time, and most of that talk was students retelling to each other. The charts in the same rooms were all about retelling, and the modeled thinking during read-aloud was just the same: retelling, not getting at the heart of what was really going on in the text. In a few of the rooms, I specifically heard teachers talking about levels and students labeling themselves by levels.

I decided to visit the classroom of Jaime, our reading specialist. When students struggled with reading, Jaime was the person everyone would turn to, and usually this would lead to the students being pulled for an extra period of forty minutes of reading support. Jaime's schedule was tight as she worked with students in every grade, and some grades, she said, had a great number of strugglers.

Lots of wheels were now spinning in my mind, but I needed some help figuring out just what all these wheels were telling me. I made a few phone calls. I was reminded of Elizabeth, the "teacher-in-the-principal's-office" in the introduction of this book. She reminded me of the importance of volume of reading. She said that the single greatest predictor of student success in reading was the amount of time they spent reading books at their level. Of course! Malcolm Gladwell! Richard Allington! Ten thousand hours of practice!

I then visited Jennie, a principal friend of mine one town over. Listening to the sound of talk in her school helped me pinpoint the need to teach into greater depth. Kindergarten and first-grade teachers were teaching children to say phrases like "That makes me think" or "That reminds me of" when talking to their partners, and the partner time was longer, sometimes double the time students were spending talking to partners in my school.

Forming a Plan

All of this made me realize I needed to provide a new type of support in my school to increase reading levels: increase the amount of time students spend reading and talking about their reading and increase the depth with which students discuss their texts, even at a very young age!

I tested the waters with the four-resources model to brainstorm various possible solutions. Although I didn't implement every idea on the chart

(I decided that the computer-based reading program was not a good fit for our school's needs or philosophy), getting all of my ideas down on paper helped me to see all of my options. (See Figure 3.12.)

FIGURE 3.12

FOUR RESOURCES MODEL FOR FINDING SOLUTIONS (SAMPLE)

Financial Resources	Human Resources	Temporal Resources	Spatial Resources
Purchase more books at levels where there may be gaps in classroom libraries.	Allow reading specialist to coach teachers on strategies to improve reading level. Cluster students reading at similar levels into classrooms for the next year.	Adjust reading specialist's schedule into thirty-minute slots instead of forty-minute slots, allowing for more slots. Adjust reading specialist's schedule to allow for more coaching of teachers. Increase amount of time on reading instruction in classroom teachers' schedules.	Establish book nooks around the school where students can go as a reward to spend extra time reading. Create a centralized lending library for teachers with many levels of text that can be borrowed.

Taking Action

Using the ideas in the chart, I worked with our staff to begin the process of transformation.

We made a number of positive changes by leveraging schedules—both the school's master schedule and the schedules that classroom teachers used for reading. First, we challenged classroom teachers to reduce the number of minutes in their minilessons and increase their reading period from forty minutes to fifty or sixty minutes. It's true that time seems to be at a premium in our classrooms, but it's amazing how teachers can indeed find time for things when they're necessary. By cutting down the number of minutes spent unpacking in the morning and reducing the transition time between other subjects, we were able to give students larger chunks of reading time each day.

We also adjusted the reading specialist's pullout periods from forty minutes to thirty minutes. Our reasons for this were twofold: First, our struggling readers often felt saturated after thirty minutes of pullout support, and second, shortening the pullout periods allowing for more periods in the specialist's day. We used the extra time for coaching in classrooms and for an additional pullout period per day for the most fragile readers.

When making the school's master schedule for the following year, we were careful not to cluster students together according to reading level. If we want our students to be reading well, our neediest readers can't be cut off from the rest of the population. Clustering of this kind would have made it easier for us to schedule in-class and pullout support, but it wouldn't have supported our overall goal of helping children to improve their reading.

We also invested in some new resources. Classroom teachers advised which levels of books were the sparsest in their classroom libraries, and we purchased books to help students have greater variety to support their volume of reading. Additionally, we kept a core of books at all levels in a community book room, where teachers and students could borrow to augment their sets, sometimes even getting second copies for partners to read together. Finally, we created book nooks around the school, small reading areas in public places where students could be sent as a reward for good behavior. One book nook has a large Snoopy figure that students can read to. Another has pup tents with flashlights. It's amazing how many more minutes of reading can be created when it's treated like a reward.

Long-Term Results

This story began to unfold a few years ago, and I've seen the landscape of reading levels and the teachers' understanding of reading instruction change tremendously! Yes, we still have struggling readers in our school, but we have a greater handle on who they are, identifying them sooner rather than later and creating structures of support. The revisions to the daily life of our school have helped us initiate a response-to-intervention model of support, where fragile learners have more opportunities to read across their day. Our school has thrived in formal means of assessment like standardized testing and the teacher and principal evaluation that are attached to it, in the sense of consistency of reading assessment and instruction across the grade levels, and, most importantly, in students' ownership of their growth as readers. We have fewer and fewer students saying things like "I'm a level M," and more and more talking about deep ideas in their books and the way they are improving their thinking.

Looking Back and Looking Ahead

Our days are filled with decisions. Some are urgent, dealing with safety, discipline, and the overall well-being of the children and adults in our care. These require thinking on the spot based on best practices. Other decisions are about learning, building community, and the long-term success of our school. The weakest leaders stifle their subordinates, afraid that giving these people power detracts from their own. The strongest leaders empower those who work for them.

Although we may not reap rewards from our decisions immediately, these decisions will have a long-lasting, positive effect on the lives of our students and the professionals who work with them.

Chapter 4

EVALUATE TO SUPPORT TEACHERS' AND STUDENTS' LEARNING

Our school had recently embarked on a study of mindset theory, the idea that people's self-identity as learners had a long-lasting impact on their success in learning. For about four months, we had studied the work of Carol Dweck, Gravity Goldberg, Kristine Mraz, and Christine Hertz. We worked on infusing language into our teaching that supported a growth mindset in students and in ourselves. It was an exciting time for this group of highly motivated teachers.

It was also time for Kristen, a teacher with a great deal of experience, to meet with me to discuss an upcoming observation. At the start of our meeting, I asked Kristen what the focus of her lesson would be. I anticipated the usual responses: reading, writing, maybe social studies. Instead, she said, "I'd like to do a lesson where I teach students about what it means to have a growth mindset in their learning."

This was exciting to me as an observer! Not only was Kristen taking her study of growth mindset seriously, but she was asking me to be a part of the study with her in what traditionally is seen as a high-risk situation: an observation. What had she and I done in the past to make her feel comfortable enough to try out something brand-new (and something she and I could really learn from) in this type of setting?

This chapter deals with this question precisely. How do we create such excitement and such trust around adult learning in our schools that teachers view observations as opportunities to grow and to receive feedback on new concepts they are exploring?

August and September: Critical Conversations for the Beginning of the Year

Few things in life cry out with such expectant anticipation as early autumn in school. Floors are waxed and shiny. Fadeless construction paper is on the backing of every bulletin board. Student names adorn the desks. Well-rested teachers tell stories of their trips or the books they've read while waiting at the copy machine. Yes, there's a buzz of eagerness on the last few days before students come back for their first day in a new grade.

You've also spent your summer preparing. You've established schedules, made sure everyone has their supplies, and thought out how you'll put your goals and those of the district into action. Part of that plan has to be around evaluation . . . and the year hasn't even really begun yet!

That's right. The year hasn't officially started, but you're already thinking about evaluation. Yes, you'll get your paperwork around observations, walk-throughs, goal-setting, and other formal parts of the process organized. However, some of your most visionary work has to happen right now through the lens of evaluation.

Having conversations in the beginning of the year is the first step on a ten-month journey of learning for your students and your teachers. These don't have to be formally scheduled, sit-down meetings. They might feel more relaxed than that, but certain factors might help you make the most of these talks.

Think about what work you have covered with your entire school or cadres of teachers recently. Andy Hargreaves and Michael Fullan (2012) tell us that although it's important to work with each teacher, differentiating and meeting individual needs, the fast track to school improvement is in working with teachers en masse, growing their skills in groups. So, when we consider evaluations, we need to keep our whole-school initiatives in mind.

How do we set reasonable expectations for our teachers in the beginning of a school year? One way is to use the staircase model of expectation. Consider something you've studied as a group (in professional learning communities, in faculty meetings, in professional development) and think of where you are in its implementation. Ask yourself about which level of understanding your teachers might be on. Have they simply been exposed to something (with a little demonstration or conversation), have they been immersed in it (guided demonstration, coaching, extended amounts of professional development time), or can we expect that they've mastered it?

The model staircase found in Figure 4.1 plots the steps of implementation around conferences in reading and writing workshop, but you can create a staircase like this for any focus or subject area. You'll notice that the staircase identifies "phases." These are the periods of development in teachers. Phases may last part of a year, a year, or several years. It's also worth noting that these phases are particular to different elements of practice, not to the teacher as a whole. A teacher may be in a "mastery" phase for some elements of practice and "exposure" for other elements.

If you've already thought about managing expectations across your school, you are ready to think about what you know about each teacher, revisiting summative evaluations from the previous year. Think about areas of strength and need. Think about goals you may have begun to set last year. Think about what overall goals you have for the entire school this year, and how this teacher might fit into that. Then, consider how you want to raise these ideas with teachers. (See Figure 4.2.)

Conversations to Build on Strength

To give you an idea of what a beginning-of-the-year conversation with a strong teacher who is looking to grow might look like in practice, here's how I began the year with Kristen, the teacher we met at the beginning of this chapter. As you saw earlier, Kristen was ready to take on a real risk in the weeks before her evaluation. This conversation may give you an idea of how we laid the groundwork for that decision.

Kristen is exceptionally good at listening closely to students. When students talk to her, she looks them in the eye, or even deeper—sometimes, I think,

STAIRCASE OF LEARNING EXAMPLE: CONFERENCES IN READING WORKSHOP

Teachers are learning

- Teacher combines students for small-group instruction based on need.
- Conferring is used as a second means of assessing students.

Teachers are implementing and approximating

- Teacher models within his or her conferences.
- Teacher compliments student on something.
- Demonstration and coaching are used as teaching methods.

Teachers are learning

- Teacher models within his or her conferences.
- Teacher compliments student on something.
- Demonstration and coaching are used as teaching methods.

Teachers are implementing and approximating

- Conferences are held regularly.
- Teaching point stated each time.
- Teacher records findings.

Teachers have mastered

- Conferences are held regularly.
- Teaching point stated each time.
- Teacher records findings.

Teachers are learning

- Conferences are held regularly.
- Teaching point stated each time.
- Teacher records findings.

EXPOSURE PHASE

Teachers are trying something new.

IMMERSION PHASE

Teachers are beyond initial experiences but still refining their work.

MASTERY PHASE

Teachers are highly skilled in this area and taking on new challenges.

FIGURE 4.2

LANGUAGE FOR INTRODUCING GOALS WITH TEACHERS

If the teacher . . .	Then, you might say . . .
Has shown great success	What are you ready for now? How can we take your work and put it into the realm of leadership?
Is new	I can't wait to work with you on ____.
Needs support in a particular area	Here's what I think you're ready for. How can I help you do that?
Has been slow to come around to something you've been working on as a school (essentials)	Let's identify what absolutely has to be in place this year. How can I help you do that?
Tends to work alone	I'd like you to work with ____ on ____.

right into their soul. She responds up close, meeting kids where they are, and pulls them up higher until they are where they need to be.

Kristen also applies new learning from professional reading and staff development, meshing her new learning with what she already knows to be good for children. Her adaptability makes her the head learner of her own classroom, and that is exactly the tone she sets.

Meeting with Kristen in the beginning of the year to set goals can be a daunting task. I especially need to find an area of interest so that she can be engaged enough to pursue something that will further improve her strengths (and those of her students, and those of her colleagues, and mine as well!).

You'll notice that I'm focusing on strengths here. I avoid approaching goal setting from a deficit model. Just as with students, it can be easy to make the mistake of trying to build a goal around an area that needs improvement. However, this provides a very weak foundation at best, one that you can't really build upon. You have to build on strengths. (Areas that need growth will be addressed in the next section.)

Kristen and I set a time to talk at the beginning of the year. We met in my office. Here's how the conversation went:

I'm digging deeper to get her to say more. This is exploratory talk.

I'm adding some of my own thinking to the conversation. Some of this adds to Kristen's content knowledge, and some of it pushes our conversation along with new ideas.

Another follow-up question. I'm building the conversation on something she said so that I point our thinking in a certain direction. Where we'll end up, I'm not exactly sure.

ME: Hi, Kristen. Happy New Year! You're coming off the summer following another great year. What are you hoping to study this year?

KRISTEN: Thanks. Math. I'd like to do something with math.

ME: Like what?

KRISTEN: I want to find a better way to enrich math for my students that really get it.

ME: What do you do now to enrich math for those students?

KRISTEN: The program gives us those enrichment sheets, but I think these kids need more than that.

ME: What do you mean?

KRISTEN: Well, the enrichment sheets are easy for these kids. They finish them up in a minute or two, and they don't really enrich their learning. It's just more of the same.

ME: Right. Kids that are good at the algorithmic part of math will speed through computation and even much of the simple problem solving, and they need something to slow down their learning, don't they? Something that will make them think, and grow their number sense.

KRISTEN: Exactly. They seem bored by something that's supposed to be enriching!

ME: That's interesting that you used the word bored. Can you say more about that?

KRISTEN: Well, these kids solve more problems that have nothing to do with them. They're just something someone else made up.

ME: Doesn't that keep the math far away from them? It makes it something that's just so foreign to their world.

KRISTEN: (Pointing!) Yes! That's it. It has nothing do with them.

ME: Just think of how important kids' writing is to them the way we teach it [in writing workshop]. We build it on top of their own lives, and their own experiences.

KRISTEN: And they never want to stop writing.

ME: Exactly. It's just so relevant to them.

KRISTEN: Even in their reading, they try to see themselves in their books. They get their own ideas and go with them.

ME: Relevance. That's a topic lots of smart people out there are talking about in learning. When kids are so removed from their learning, it's like watching the learning on a movie screen, like a shadow of learning. You can't help but be passive in learning like that.

KRISTEN: And that's not how we try to teach here. We try to get kids involved in their work. We try to get them talking, to be hands-on, to use manipulatives, to tell their stories.

ME: I think we know what you want to study this year: relevance.

KRISTEN: (Nods)

ME: How do we make learning relevant?

KRISTEN: I came here thinking we were going to talk about math, and only for those top students.

ME: Right. This is so much bigger than that, isn't it? Imagine the impact this is going to have on you and your students for the rest of your life. You're really ready for this.

KRISTEN: Right. Let's get started.

> *Hearing Kristen's excitement about this idea lets me know that we've hit on something that energizes her. Making this a discussion of what she might focus on this year, not an announcement of what I think she should focus on this year, gives her ownership and agency in the work to come.*

> *Giving this idea a clear name helps us to define the plan. I also underscore how this idea is urgent, and, well, relevant.*

> *We give the study a working title to establish the direction of her work. This title can also come from the teacher. This is often the case with these conversations: when people have an opportunity to talk through their ideas, they often deepen their thinking.*

> *In my experience, the phrase "You're ready for this" is powerful when talking to teachers about next steps. It communicates faith in the teacher and a sense of challenge.*

Following this portion of the conversation, Kristen and I brainstormed about some professional texts and other resources including teachers she might visit and language she might integrate into her lessons. We also talked about how I might support her in this study, especially with time and financial resources. We discussed how we can use our observations this year as a sounding board for Kristen's work around relevance, and already I see that I'll be conducting my walk-throughs and observations with the lens of relevance in mind.

Conversations to Nudge Beyond Compliance

Not all of these conversations are quite so smooth. Kristen is a highly engaged teacher, who reflects on her practice and always tries to outdo herself. She applies new learning from professional development and seeks out her own learning opportunities, studying her students and many resources to refine her practice.

There are also teachers who are just compliant. These are teachers who implement mandates, just enough, but don't take on robust plans for improvement. These teachers may be hesitant to implement new practices because they feel self-conscious about their own abilities in a particular area. Or perhaps they're buying time in the belief that the proverbial pendulum will eventually swing the other way. Whatever the reason, compliant teachers may bring less enthusiasm to these beginning-of-the-year meetings than a risk-taking teacher like Kristen does.

Jennifer is a second-grade teacher in another school. She has taught second grade for many years.

Jennifer is very good at classroom management. She has presented at conferences about her practice. Although she loves a well-run classroom, Maggie, her principal, notices that even in her orderly, fastidiously designed space, Jennifer doesn't really hone in close to listen to her students' understandings of what she's taught. Maggie and Jennifer's school has adopted many student-driven methodologies to teaching: independent reading, discovery-oriented math, and elements of play and choice throughout the students' day.

Maggie is concerned that although the district has focused on student-driven methodologies for years, Jennifer seems to be the lone holdout in her practices. Her teaching, on its surface, seems to be solid: the pacing of the lesson is appropriate. She's activating schema at the beginning of the lesson and providing closure at the end of the lesson. The kids are quiet and smiling. But Jennifer is not highly responsive to her students' needs: she's teaching what she's always taught, even though it's not what her current students need. Her instruction is not differentiated: for example, she's teaching *every* kid blends, even though most of the kids in class already know this. Although this might seem innocuous, it's teaching the kids to be passive and to fake their way through school.

Here's an excerpt from the conversation with Jennifer. You'll see that there are two main lines of thinking in Maggie's comments: one that accentuates her strengths in the area of management, and another about areas of concern.

MAGGIE: Hi, Jennifer. We're ready for another great year.

JENNIFER: Yes, it's going to be great.

MAGGIE: You developed really nice behavioral systems in your class last year. You presented at the conference in New York and shared your learning at two faculty meetings. These are big steps for you.

> *Maggie starts by naming good things Jennifer did.*

JENNIFER: Yes, it was great.

MAGGIE: What are you hoping to do to build on this in the new year?

> *Maggie gives Jennifer the chance to start the conversation with the expectation that she will grow this year.*

JENNIFER: I'm not so sure.

MAGGIE: You have a great amount of expertise when it comes to behavior. How can we share your learning and your excitement with others?

JENNIFER: I can talk at a faculty meeting again.

MAGGIE: That would be great. I also think people would get so much out of seeing you in action. Have you ever thought about taking on some leadership in the form of science coaching?

> *Jennifer thinks about repeating last year's work. Maggie pushes her gently out of this comfort zone to boost her engagement in something that she already feels confident with.*

JENNIFER: Me? A coach?

MAGGIE: Yes. People are already used to being coached in literacy by Heather. Why not try that out?

JENNIFER: When would I do that?

MAGGIE: I'm not sure. We could open it up to teachers who want to work with you, so there's no pressure on others to participate.

> *Even though Maggie doesn't have all the answers to the logistics, she starts with the substance.*

JENNIFER: I'm not really sure how to coach.

MAGGIE: Take a look at this book on instructional coaching. This chapter right here talks about ways to work with adults in a classroom setting. I can also arrange time for you to work with Heather on how she does it.

> *Maggie offers Jennifer some support to make her feel more comfortable. Even if the coaching never happens, reading the chapter and talking to Heather will help Maggie to grow as a professional.*

JENNIFER: (Sounding interested) When would I do this?

MAGGIE: I could probably find a way for you to get coverage.

JENNIFER: Hmm, sounds interesting.

Maggie brings up the elephant in the room. There are essential things missing from Jennifer's teaching. Notice how Maggie doesn't open it up for a philosophical discussion, but gives Jennifer a voice in the type of support she'd like to get this done this year.

MAGGIE: We're also trying to tie this year's goals into last year's learning. During your summative conference last year, we talked about student-driven instruction. There are some essentials we named that we've been studying as a school for a few years now: listening closely to students, using formal and informal data, and thinking of ways to group students together based on their needs. These are things we've identified as a school as critical to instruction, but things you said you need some more support to make happen in your class. What can I do to help you make this all happen this year?

JENNIFER: I really need some more modeling.

Maggie digs deeper. This implies depth from her as a supervisor and her expectations of Jennifer.

Maggie creates professional partnerships as well as structures of time to make it happen.

MAGGIE: What specifically do you feel you need more support with?

JENNIFER: Student conferences. I have trouble naming what a student needs to learn.

MAGGIE: We can certainly set up a study of this. I'll arrange some time for you with Heather, and I'll get you coverage to work with Bridget, who is so adept at conferences.

JENNIFER: That'd be great.

Maggie now tucks in a deadline as a benchmark. By tying it to an observation, she reminds Jennifer of her growth's importance to her evaluation. As the conversation continues, Maggie addresses some of the other areas that were in need of improvement, setting up a timeline of benchmarks throughout the year.

MAGGIE: I'll make these arrangements this week, and we should make it a goal that it can be one of the focuses of your observation in November. At that point, we can check in on this and see what other support you need.

Conversations to Address Noncompliance

Kristen and Jennifer represent two types of teachers. One is engaged in her own learning, constantly bettering herself in the name of learning and in the name of her students. The second is compliant, simply content with what she knows. Please note that Jennifer's seeming lack of engagement does not mean that she cares less for her students. Her vision of teaching and learning are just different. At their heart, all teachers care for their students. When we as leaders stop recognizing this or trying to identify it in teachers, we begin to lose the hope that is necessary for us in our work.

However, other teachers refuse to comply with the demands of teaching and learning. These noncompliant teachers simply won't do what is asked of them. These are the teachers that challenge us to identify their dedication to students. However, just as Jennifer's view of teaching and learning is different from Kristen's, noncompliant teachers' perspective is even more divergent than what we might see as the cycle of learning. Even so, we must work to figure out just *why* they refuse to comply and *what* they believe in.

My friend and colleague Eric works in another district. The quotes found in Figure 4.3 are things teachers said to him and his principal colleagues in the weeks just before this chapter was written. It is easy to be blinded by the apparent resistance in these statements. However, we can achieve greater success when we try to name what is behind them.

When we look at noncompliant teachers through these lenses, it can humanize them. We might see their insecurities and their misunderstandings. Immediately, that makes them easier for us to teach and to lead. By identifying what they value, we find an avenue into their learning, just as we did with Kristen and Jennifer earlier in this chapter. (It just might be harder for us to identify, because we're distracted by the power struggle that is often associated with noncompliance.)

Eric and his colleagues have developed eight strategies to help guide these teachers along a continuum of self-improvement in practice.

1. **Empowerment**. Part of the struggle of compliance is about power. There's an invisible tug-of-war about who knows what's best for students. When we allow the teacher to have a voice in

FIGURE 4.3

IDENTIFYING THE BELIEFS OF NON-COMPLIANT TEACHERS

Statement	What's Under the Surface	What This Teacher Might Believe
I have done it this way for twenty years.	Possible fear that a new system might be inferior. Worry that prior practice might be challenged, and previously taught students may have been misled.	Teaching traditions equal best practice.
This doesn't work with my students.	Possible fear that something might cause disequilibrium of control.	Teachers need to be in control of the classroom. Lack of control is threatening to the teacher.
My students can't do this. It is too hard.	Possible disbelief in the ability of students.	Teachers should only provide instruction that is safe to implement and that students will master immediately.
We don't have the materials to implement this.	Possible anxiety related to lack of preparedness.	Teaching practice must be perfect.
The person who wrote this curriculum didn't know my children.	Possible lack of trust in experts. Possible disbelief in the ability of students.	The teacher's students have very unique needs that only the teacher can understand.
There is too much to do (initiative overload).	A natural sense of being overwhelmed.	One more new thing extends beyond the teacher's abilities and the abilities of the students.
I just don't think I'm ready to implement this. I'm not sure how it goes. I need more training.	Possible anxiety related to lack of preparedness.	There is always a right way and a wrong way to teach. The teacher can only implement it once she knows it's perfect.
I tried this and it doesn't work.	Underestimation of the complexity of the task.	The teacher tried it once, but it didn't work. Something must be wrong with it. The teacher is a solid teacher. If it didn't work for him, it can't be good.

naming best practice, the teacher feels heard and might be more ready to hear us. Ask the teacher some of the following to confront the issue, and not avoid it.

- What would you recommend and why?
- What would you do differently?
- How can we customize this to your comfort level or your strength?
- Are you able to work in a safe place to take professional risks and learn from your possible mistakes?

2. **Fostering collegiality.** Working with partners helps anyone in a learning situation address questions and doubts. When you allow teachers to work together with partners on the practice in question, it also reassures them that they are not alone in the work. Help them study the practice with others, but establish the norm that whatever new thinking comes from the partnership, dissolution of the practice is not an option.

3. **Leader as model.** When you roll up your sleeves and try out what you're asking the teachers to try, you show them that the work can be done and that you're willing to risk your own vulnerability to try it. Involve the teacher in the planning and the evaluation. Invite feedback from the teacher, and ask her to apply the feedback as well when teaching the students. Eventually, you might evolve this practice into a coteaching setting with her.

4. **Professional development.** You should never expect a teacher to do something that hasn't been taught (just as you wouldn't expect students to do something that wasn't taught). The greatest success comes from job-embedded, sustained professional development with a consistent person. We also must expect that different teachers will have different levels of buy-in after each professional development experience. People's compliance-related anxiety often comes from a lack of exposure or confidence in their own content knowledge. Building this up is critical to move toward engagement.

5. **Proficient partner.** It's inevitable that some noncompliant teachers have the mindset of teachers versus administrators. Pairing up a noncompliant teacher with an unofficial mentor with a slightly better skill set can help the noncompliant teacher see how something might work. Seeing and hearing a colleague experiencing success can be a great support to the noncompliant teacher.

6. **Lab site visits.** Present noncompliant teachers as researchers who visit the classrooms of their colleagues. Try to avoid calling the lab site host a "model classroom," because this can cause animosity and resentment, as opposed to the collegiality that is essential to positive school change. Researchers should be encouraged to take notes (sometimes on heavily scaffolded note-taking guide sheets to provide lenses; see Chapter 1) and then discuss their observations with the host teacher.

7. **Nonevaluative learning walks.** Ask the noncompliant teacher to set goals before the walk begins. Ask him to think about what he hopes to see and what he'd like feedback on. This provides a focus. While in the rooms, the teacher and the principal should chart what is seen and then debrief it in a positive way, discussing application of new concepts and the expectations associated with them.

8. **Collaborative plans.** Create a plan together with the teacher. Leaving the teacher out of the plan will probably cause further resistance to it.

   - Set small, attainable goals with feasible deadlines.
   - Celebrate success, and plan subsequent goals based on these.

Walk-throughs

Another piece of the teacher evaluation pie is the evaluative walk-through. This is different from the learning visits described in Chapter 1. The purpose of this walk-through is to gather data that will feed into the final evaluation. Some models use judgmental (positive or negative) language during the walk-through, and others simply use it to gather data that will be judged at the end of the year. Whichever model you and your district use, you can employ this time in the classroom to lead toward growth for the teacher.

The walk-through is the tool that can most easily be applied as a "gotcha," to catch noncompliant teachers who are not keeping up with mandates: You can hold teachers to things that should be expectations based on the teachers' years of experience or their level of exposure to certain practices. However, "gotcha" management isn't something we aim for. The following list gives suggestions on how to use the structure of the walk-through to instead push teachers to new levels of growth.

- When watching the instruction or reading the classroom, look for evidence of professional growth. This might be the application of recommendations you've made in the past, ideas that were studied together in professional development or professional reading, or things you've discussed in faculty meetings.

- If you're studying something as a school (like the idea of growth mindset as shared in the opening vignette of the chapter), you can tell your teachers that the walk-throughs during part of the year will focus on their attempts in this area. You can add momentum to the study by celebrating their approximations within the walk-throughs, noting their misconceptions and addressing what you noticed at a future faculty meeting or professional development session.

- As noted in Chapter 3, look for trends and patterns across the school, so that you can plan the necessary next steps for a particular area of professional study.

- Jane Bean-Folkes, my former colleague at the Teachers College Reading and Writing Project, sometimes leaves a sticky note in the classroom with a compliment so the teacher has some immediate written (and therefore permanent) feedback on things that are done well.

- Gossip productively about great things you see. For example, visit a neighboring teacher, the nurse—anyone who'll listen—and say something nice about something you just saw. Of course, you'll have to determine for yourself the impact this might have. If it creates excitement, do it. If it creates hidden (or not so hidden) animosity, refrain from this.

- Whether the judgment happens in the write-up, in a follow-up conversation, or in the summative evaluation at the end of the year, try to include *because* clauses, explaining why something is a strength.

Observations

Observations once had a disproportionately large piece of the teacher evaluation pie. For many tenured teachers, it was the annual visit from the supervisor. Everything would be packed into that one visit, and much of the supervisor's summative evaluation of the teacher would be based on this one thirty- to forty-minute lesson. *One and done. Dog and pony show. The gotcha!* These were words teachers used to use to describe this experience, which was probably one of the most anxious moments of the school year and didn't amount to much reflection or growth for either the teacher or the observer.

The advent of reform in teacher evaluation calls for more (sometimes *many* more) formal interactions between teacher and principal. When this change first occurred, it brought with it greater anxiety. Of course it did, because of the natural nervousness that comes when company is coming. However, it's also opened up many new doors of conversation between teachers and their leaders to reflect and learn—and learning is what teachers do best, isn't it? Instead of focusing on the natural nervousness in anticipation of company coming, we can create cultures in which we place the emphasis on the joy of the visit when loved ones are around. To help teachers make the shift from feeling nervous about observations to feeling excited about them, we can remind them how teaching in front of others (which we'll do our fair share of also!) helps school communities rally around practices that help children. All this is true—if it's done right!

And *you*, as the head learner, can make that happen!

Preparing for the Observation

When we confer with students in a reading and writing workshop, we often open up the conference with what Carl Anderson calls the research part (2000). We start by watching the student in action, by looking over the notes of previous conferences, and by asking questions. We look for something we can complement and something we can teach. This helps us hone in on strengths that we can build on. It helps us set goals that are built not on deficits or weaknesses, but on assets that can be enhanced through good teaching. The act of researching helps us deliver highly differentiated teaching to each student. Another truly magical part of this part of the conference is that the student has a direct role in establishing the context for what is about to be learned. The student has a say in what will be learned. This is perhaps why Katie Wood Ray and Lester Laminack call conferring the "essential teaching act" in *Writing Workshop: Working Through the Hard Parts, and They're All Hard Parts* (2001).

The same is true when we observe teachers. Observations, like conferences, can be the essential teaching act in the career of a teacher. They can be the opportunity we have to build the best possible teacher. So, like Carl Anderson's model, we need to begin the observation before the observation, by doing our research.

In our meetings with teachers before announced observations, we can start by reviewing previous observations and evaluations. Because we want our teachers to continually grow just like our students, we have to take notice of the work of previous visits to build on strengths and recommendations that were noted or discussed. We can also talk about things we've noticed in our learning visits. The following questions are responsive, yet open-ended in nature, and allow the teacher to also have a voice in setting the table for the observation.

- During our last observation, we talked about _____. How's that going? How can we build on that?

- One of your learning goals for this year is _____. How might this observation support your learning in that?

- When I visited your room last week, one thing that struck me was _____. How can we explore that somehow in this next observation?

- What has the learning of this class pushed you into thinking about lately? How can we explore that somehow in this next observation?

- One thing I've seen you doing lately is (name a strength). I'd like to grow that some more with you. How can we use this observation to help you with that?

The preconference is also a time where you can discuss the norms for the observation that will follow. When choosing subject matter for the observation, consider what might help the teacher grow the most. Sometimes this decision is made by the observer. Sometimes it can be made together with the teacher. Remember that this can be an area of strength (because you can always build on a strength) or an area of need (when you're dealing with an emergency on with noncompliance). (See Figure 4.4.)

FIGURE 4.4

WHAT YOU CHOOSE TO OBSERVE MAY INDICATE WHAT YOU VALUE	
If you choose to observe . . .	**You might support . . .**
The teacher teaching in a prescriptive, scripted program your school uses	Conformity and fidelity to a program
A lesson that is highly differentiated	The teacher's ability to make instructional decisions
A specific age group or subject area	The teacher's content knowledge about that age group or subject area
An inquiry lesson	The intensity with which teachers listen closely to their students, or levels of student thinking

When deciding on what will be observed, also take into consideration your conversation from the beginning of the year. What goals did you set that can be supported through an observation at this point in the year? If you and the teacher set a professional goal, you should revisit it during the observation, at least tangentially. You can decide, based on the time of the year, what your expectation is within this goal. Is it something that should be mastered? If not, what expectations can you and the teacher set about this goal during the lesson you'll observe? When you use the observation as a time to check in on these goals, you give life to the timeline of professional learning.

Another important factor to figure out is what role you'll play when you're observing, because that will affect the exact kind of feedback you'll give. For example, if you observe a teacher as a fly on the wall, you can objectively transcribe what you see and hear and then discuss it later. If you choose to coach through a part of the lesson, you'll be trying to help the teacher internalize the language of certain teaching modalities, and the immediate feedback within the moment will help the teacher retain new learning.

Teacher evaluation law in many states requires that at least some of the observations be unannounced. Going in to observe teachers without advanced notice doesn't mean going in cold. You yourself will probably want to prepare so that the observation can still serve as a meaningful experience for you and the teacher. To do that:

- Reread previous observations and decide on a subject area, special class, or area of practice you'd like to observe the teacher in.

- Think about individual, group, school, or district goals you're hoping the teacher can demonstrate in the classroom.

- Look at the teacher's schedule to make sure that when you show up, he is teaching something that will reflect these ideas.

- Read the teacher's lesson plans to find the lesson that will best reflect areas of potential growth for the teacher.

During the Observation

Company's coming! In all likelihood, the teacher is nervous. You yourself should feel nervous, too, but in a positive, excited sort of way. You are about to put yourself in the company of learning on so many levels. Students will be learning something about math, science, reading, writing, social studies . . . something. A teacher will be learning about deepening her practice. And if it's done right, you'll be learning from all of them: about the content, about the practice, and about how you can help all of it grow through your leadership.

Depending on the role you've mutually decided upon with the teacher, you'll do different things. If you've decided to be a fly-on-the-wall observer, you'll record what the teacher is doing. This record keeping depends on the model of teacher observation your district has chosen. This might include highly scaffolded checklists or a very open-ended model for you to record what you see and hear. However, the learning lens you use to watch this lesson will depend on the roles you and the teacher have chosen.

Even though the various teacher observation models that districts use (Danielson, Marshall, Marzano, McREL, Stronge) vary in their execution (time frame, frequency, method of recording), each has at its heart student learning and teacher practice. Whether you're following a guided checklist or a more narrative form, you're going to notice things about the instruction, about the student work, and about the room that stand out to you about the teacher's work. What you see and hear will lead you to wonderings and conclusions. Certain observation models will want you to record these thoughts and observations, and others will ask you to hold them for post-observation conferences, subsequent observations, or final evaluations. Figure 4.5 might help you find the words that will help you consider.

Before the observation, decide—with the teacher, and if the rules of your particular model allow you—what your role will be. If you've decided to coach during the observation, there are a number of ways in which to do this. Remember that an observation is often an anxious situation, so any coaching should be done by coaching lightly, not pushing too hard. Following are a few strategies.

FIGURE 4.5

CONSIDERING WHAT YOU SEE IN AN OBSERVATION

If you see . . .	The issue might be . . .	You might wonder . . .	And here's how you might move forward . . .
Something that reflects professional learning	The teacher is gesturing toward, is playing with, or has mastered the learning.	How well did the teacher internalize the new learning? What would be good next steps?	The teacher can continue to grow in this learning by ___.
The teacher misunderstanding professional learning	The teacher is challenged by ___.	Where did the teacher's understanding fall apart? (Possible trouble spots include miscommunication at professional development sessions, misunderstanding in professional learning communities, misapplication with these students.) Does the teacher realize there is a problem?	The teacher should work to deepen understanding about ___.
A strong continuation of previous professional learning	The teacher is very reflective.	What replicable steps did this teacher take that others could take also?	The teacher can deepen the learning or share it by _____.

continues

Nonverbal Cues. Give encouragement and guidance through nonverbal cues. Decide on these cues with the teacher before the observation. They might include thumbs-up, a smile, or a nod. You can also create hand gestures together with the teacher that mean "I'm not sure that worked," "You should go back and try that again," or "Watch that student."

Read the Room. This can be especially good when the teacher wants feedback with a bird's-eye view of the class as a whole. During a moment of transition, stand together with the teacher and say,

CONSIDERING WHAT YOU SEE IN AN OBSERVATION, *cont.*

If you see . . .	The issue might be . . .	You might wonder . . .	And here's how you might move forward . . .
Unusual classroom arrangement	The teacher is investigating alternative structures to the environment. The students' behavior or learning has prompted a change in the room arrangement.	How does this arrangement affect the learning in this room?	The teacher can reflect on how the arrangement of the room is helping learning. Depending on the reflection, the teacher might change the arrangement or try other solutions.
Behavior problems	The students are not engaged because of the content or presentation. The teacher needs greater support in behavior management.	Why are the students behaving this way?	The teacher can research or work with a coach to learn new behavioral or instructional strategies to use in the classroom.
Something that the teacher stumbled on that works well	This is a reflective or instinctually strong teacher in some way.	How did the teacher figure this out? How does it promote learning?	The teacher can reflect on this success, asking: How can we share this with others? How can we build on this strength?

"What do you notice?," "Look at those students right there," or "Let's listen in right here." Ask the teacher to name conclusions, and help her understand what you think might be happening. After reading the room, set the teacher up for a next step, which might be responding to the classroom management (positive or negative) or simply continuing with instruction.

Provide Immediate Feedback. During a moment of transition, talk about a teaching move the teacher just made. This is especially important if it's an area the teacher mentioned as a goal during the pre-observation conference. Fresh-out-of-the-oven feedback is much more effective right there in the moment than feedback that has been given a day or two to cool off. It also allows a teacher to see the immediate result of what just happened instructionally. Giving feedback in the moment also allows a chance to remediate on the spot.

Whisper In. If you choose to whisper in (see Chapter 2 for more about this strategy), position yourself in a place where the teacher can easily hear you. Listen in as the teacher starts teaching, and freeze the conversation (or allow the teacher to freeze the conversation) with a time-out whenever necessary. You might provide some of the language the teacher might use, or help her make decisions about how to respond to what the student is doing. Remember, this is coaching lightly, so if you've given multiple prompts, you might want to say, "Try that, and I'm going to move over. Let me know how it goes." Give the teacher some space and listen from afar. In a minute or two, ask the teacher to give you a reflection. When documenting whispered-in coaching, write what the teacher did with your guidance. This honors the learning of the teacher, and allows him to try out new teaching moves without the risk.

After the Observation

Once your visit is over, it is up to you to write the thank-you card: the write-up with feedback from the visit. This document should feel less like a product and more like part of a larger process. It is an important tool in the growth of a teacher, but it is not the only tool. It is also an invitation to the teacher for a conversation about the visit. Depending on the model you follow, you may or may not have a choice in which comes first, the thank-you card (the write-up of the observation) or the return invitation (meeting with the teacher to discuss the lesson). If you have a choice on which comes first, you might consider if there are still many questions in your mind about what you saw. If so, you might want to meet before you write up the lesson and share it. If you're pretty sure you understand what you saw, you might choose to write up the lesson and then meet.

In the days of more traditional observations, these meetings were called "postobservation conferences" or "debriefings." A slightly different spin on these chats is to call them "growth conversations."

During growth conversations, we start by asking open-ended questions, avoiding questions that lead to value judgments. Questions like, "How do you think the lesson went?" tend to lead to labels that bear judgments: *fine, okay, good, great.* Instead, if you keep the conversation about learning, the growth will never really end. Try some of these nonjudgmental questions as conversation starters:

- What did you learn during this lesson?
- What did you discover about yourself as a teacher?
- How did this visit help you in your study of _____ this year?
- How does this visit set you up for future learning?
- In what ways did this visit change who you are as a teacher?

Allow the teacher to talk, and know that his answers will not necessarily match what you have in mind. That's OK. You'll have a chance to address your own opinions during the conversation. Even in the midst of the conversation, avoid judgmental language. (See Figure 4.6.)

Some other things to consider:

- If you feel wary about the various roles you can take during the observation, have a conversation with others in your district. You shouldn't violate any rules, but having a conversation about the process that ensures consistency and maximizes learning for the teacher will help. If you are limited by the parameters of the system you use, try to see which of the suggestions found here *can* be used, or find *other ways* you might be able to make observations meaningful learning experiences for your teachers.

FINDING THE RIGHT LANGUAGE IN DISCUSSING AN OBSERVATION

If you want to address . . .	You might say . . .
Something you felt was very good practice	Do you know what you did? (Then name it.)
Something that was a concern	Something I noticed was ___. Can you talk to me about that?
A pattern in the teaching (positive or negative)	___ number of times during the lesson ___ happened. Let's talk through that.
Something surprising	I saw ___. Can you tell me why that happened?
Something that impressed you	You did ___. How did you do that?
A time you whispered in and the teacher followed through	Something we explored together was ___. How did that go for you?
Feedback you provided during the lesson	We talked about ___. Let's explore that some more.
An overarching, yearlong goal	This year, we're working on ___. How did this lesson fit into your growth in that?

- Depending on the model you're using, you may or may not be able to infuse your interpretation into the written observation report. Even if you can't write your thoughts down in the official evaluation, note them as a part of the learning profile of this teacher and address these thoughts in your growth conversation and in setting up for future observations.

- Think about how this observation fits into the growth of this teacher across the year (or across his career). What steps will you and the teacher create between this observation and the next one that might lead to attainment of professional goals by the end of the year?

- When you see something that is an area of need, think about how you can possibly tap into a strength of the teacher to help. For example, if the teacher has trouble recognizing long-term patterns in student work but is a great record keeper, work with her on how to use her anecdotal and assessment data to see trends in student learning.

The Cycle of Expectation

There are topics that return in students' learning lives every year. In reading, they'll read nonfiction every year. As writers, they might explore a study of personal narrative from kindergarten on up. In math, we add and subtract every year, just at varying degrees of complexity. The skills that are introduced in one grade must stand on the shoulders of the skills in the previous grade. With that, expectations also increase.

We are blown away when first- or second-grade writers write several long sentences in a row to tell their stories. We celebrate the mastery of multiplication facts in third grade. We applaud young readers for being able to restate what they've read, adding their own thoughts. However, we celebrate a little bit less when high school students tell us what 3×3 is, or if they've written a couple of sentences during the class period.

Teachers also go through phases of development, which involve their own milestones, celebrations, and expectations that they'll push themselves further and further. For example, if a first- or second-year teacher provides smooth transition between two activities, we might recognize that in an observation. However, if a teacher has been teaching for more than 5 years, we have to expect that she is doing deeper development work in her learning community.

What we choose to recognize during their observations leads to teachers' future growth. Figure 4.7 includes some sample teacher learning progressions to give you an idea how a teacher might progress in understanding, as our sense of expectation also progresses.

Each of the examples in Figure 4.7 shows a tiered development across time. These phases are not tied to specific amounts of time. Not all teachers in years 1–3 of their careers will be in phase 1 of this chart. Some teachers' learning will crystallize almost immediately, and others for a variety of reasons will plateau at a certain phase for a longer time. Also, you can probably imagine how certain topics will continue to develop into phase 4, phase 5, phase 20, depending on the vivaciousness of the learning community you lead. You can design this learning together with teachers or on your own, and you need this vision to keep even your most experienced or most talented teachers actively engaged in their own learning. The more motivated the teacher, the greater voice she might have in this process, although even your newest or neediest teachers should have at least a little voice in these decisions as well.

FIGURE 4.7

SAMPLE GOALS FOR TEACHERS			
Area to Consider	**Goals for Teachers Who Are Still Developing Their Skills in This Area (Phase 1)**	**Goals for Teachers Who Have Some Experience in This Area (Phase 2)**	**Goals for Teachers Who Are Accomplished in This Area (Phase 3)**
Classroom management	Provide smooth transitions, use positive reinforcement.	Develop a sense of community through rituals.	Create a sense of shared power, carefully balancing control and independence.
Conferences in workshop instruction	Hold conferences and record what was taught.	Balance conferring with small-group instruction.	Maintain a logical flow to what has been taught so that students add on to learning.
Questioning	Ask open-ended questions.	Follow up on student responses, listening closely and asking follow-up questions.	Teach students to question their own strategies.
Differentiation	Provide differentiated activities to teach the same thing.	Use assessment data to determine what students will need to learn.	Allow student choice in how they'll learn a task.

Summative Evaluation

April and May are very busy times in school. For many of us, testing is in the air. The temperature is rising, leading to all sorts of unrest attached to the anticipation of summer. Planning is already underway for the work of next year with the creation of class lists and schedules. And it's summative season!

In days of yore, summative evaluations were more paperwork to be done. In obligatory meetings, teachers would meet with principals and talk about their work over the entire year, largely based on a single observation if they were tenured. However, this has changed a great deal since the introduction of new teacher evaluation law and the practices that come with it.

Much like the meetings that might follow observations, these summative meetings—and the documentation that goes along with them—are growth conversations, leading to even better teaching during the next year. Some of the teacher evaluation models avoid judgmental language until this point and only now introduce categories like *effective*, *highly effective*, *partially effective*, or *ineffective*, but these are based on much more evidence than before.

Just as with the observation report, depending on the model you use, you may or may not have choice as to which happens first—the written summative evaluation or the growth conference that accompanies it. If you have the choice and are hoping for greater teacher input, you may opt to meet with the teacher first. However, if you do this, you'll also need to make sure you're including the teacher's input in the final report. You also have to consider that you might need one more meeting to discuss the report after it's shared.

When writing summative evaluations, we can look back on the goals set in the beginning of the year. Ask yourself: Were these goals met? Partially met? Changed because of the work of the year? Not addressed at all? Using these goals as a lens, think about them as you comb through your observation reports, citing how what was noted in observations and learning visits and walk-throughs addressed the goals.

When we meet, how do we keep these conversations focused on growth? We look back a little, but look ahead more. When working with teachers who need improvement, we talk about our hopes for the next year. We might name the areas in which we want them to make some changes and name those changes during this meeting, offering support.

Ways to offer support to teachers who need to make some changes:

- **Coaching.** Arrange some time with a coach, a proficient colleague, or yourself to work with the teacher right in the classroom. For specifics on how to make this work, see Chapter 2.

- **Supplies.** Sometimes materials help teachers grow in their learning. It might be books, technology, or something else.

- **Work with colleagues.** Set up some time for teachers to work together in or out of the classroom on the issue.

- **Professional development.** This can be professional reading, work with a consultant, workshops, or work with other teachers as a whole group or in small groups.

- **Time.** Providing coverage for a teacher to do some work in the area may make a difference. Think creatively about manipulating schedules, utilizing substitutes, or other ways to make this happen.

- **Space.** You could set up a space in the school for professional learning, or you could help the teacher figure out a way to use his own space more effectively.

For teachers who are doing great work, we can start conversations off by looking ahead with "What's next for you?" This conversation is an exciting one to have. It can lead to goal-setting that allows for very innovative practice. Ideas for pushing a strong teacher forward might include:

- mentoring a student teacher

- engaging in professional writing that might lead to publication

- changing a teacher's assignment

- taking on a leadership role as a teacher

The Benefits of Successful Evaluations: Success for Kids

It's May. Kristen and I are sitting down again to talk about her year. Our study of mindset theory led her to an exploration of relevance in student learning, which sprang into other topics, including student choice. She engaged her students in a greater range of academic and procedural choice, increasing her first graders' ownership and agency.

During our summative evaluation conference, Kristen reflected that by taking a step back and "handing the keys over to the students," she was able to involve them more in the important learning work of the classroom. As her supervisor, I have seen a subtle yet dramatic shift in her classroom environment, from being student centered to student driven, where students play a large part in the decision making of the class in many ways.

"I don't feel like I'm done though," Kristen says in our meeting. "I'm thinking of new ways I'll make the beginning of my year different." The work of engagement, of relevance, of student-driven classrooms, and yes, of teaching as a whole is rich, uncharted territory, something that can't be covered in the span of just one year. It's all a deep, three-dimensional journey with pathways in many directions, waiting to be uncovered. Our work this year has provided us a map for where Kristen will go next.

Chapter 5

UNITE AND LEAD THE SCHOOL COMMUNITY WITH LEARNING THEMES

A circle of children gathers. In the circle sits Nicky, a second grader. He clasps a large rock that he's painted yellow. He holds it up, saying, "My rock was writing this year. I remember my teacher used to say, 'Use more detail,' but I was afraid to do that, because I didn't think I could spell the words right."

Nodding, Amelia, the fourth grader and oldest student in the circle, says, "Thanks, Nick. Who wants to go next?" Shreya, a kindergartner, holds up a red rock, which seems bigger than she can lift easily. "Math used to scare me," she says, "because I always counted on my fingers." The others listen, as she continues. "I worked really hard, and now I can add really big numbers."

"I know what you mean," says David, a third grader holding his green rock. "My rock is about math, too." Everyone turns to listen. "I used to just freeze up whenever I saw a word problem, because all the words confused me. My teacher helped me break problems down, and now they don't scare me."

This circle of children is surrounded by similar circles with children bearing beautifully painted rocks. Each student had been asked to bring in a rock from home, painted a color that matches his or her grade level. The students were asked to think about what their rock represented—something that used to be a problem for them in their learning.

Even teachers had their purple rocks, representing new learning from this year, a student with unique needs, new curriculum that took a while to figure out, an unrelenting parent. At the end of the sharing sessions in small circles, the entire school, students and teachers alike, went outside to lay down these rocks, forming a walking bridge that spanned the length of our garden. The rainbow bridge represented learning this past year, a bridge that will last for many years to come.

At the end of the ceremony, second-grader Jack turned to his father, who had also been a student in the school and who had come to volunteer that day, asking him, "Daddy, where's your rock from when you were in second grade here?"

The Power of Metaphors

The preceding story took place on the second to last day of the school year. All year, the entire school had thought about bridges—how they connect us to others, how they are built to bring things together. It seemed fitting that an end-of-the-year celebration be a bridge-building one that looked back on the growth and learning of the past year.

Another scene about a century and a half earlier depicts a middle-aged Abraham Lincoln addressing the citizens of Illinois, and perhaps noting a broader audience, the American people. Calling on a Biblical symbol that had been used again and again by St. Augustine, Thomas Hobbes, Thomas Paine, and many others, he lyrically says, "A house divided against itself cannot stand." In this speech, the former Congressman who was running for senator in 1858 was talking about our nation, torn over the question of slavery. Like many other leaders before and since him, Lincoln knew that symbols, metaphors, and imagery are powerful tools to teach and inspire others to follow him.

There is great power in metaphors; they often give shape to things that can be difficult to define. We learn about the unknown by comparing it to the known. Lincoln was in pursuit of national unification, stating it in a way that his countrymen could understand and embrace. School leaders work toward the pursuit of learning for both students and their teachers in a way that brings both understanding and engagement. In your work as a learning leader, symbols give you the power to make abstractions about learning and growing concrete.

Metaphors also make learning more memorable, bringing a little bit of eternity to it. Experience and imagery create an imprint in our minds, and when we attach new learning to these images, they last, and we can feel their importance.

Carrying a single metaphor across an entire year can also provide a context that ties together seemingly unrelated experiences and information. It creates an excitement when we launch a new metaphor in the fall, and a magic when we look back on it in the late spring. The single metaphor helps relay the message that our learning is one big project, not a random collection of small efforts. By doing so, it makes our learning seem like a much more important venture, one that is always ongoing.

One aspect of leadership that has experienced renewal is that of establishing community within schools and districts. Many fields from marketing to religion have worked to distinguish between *crowds* (groups of people, united for a finite period of time, because of a short-term goal) and *communities* (groups of people who share a vision, united for an extended period of time, because of a long-term goal). Principals and other learning leaders need to establish communities around student and professional learning to sustain success for themselves and those who follow them for the long term.

When a school gathers around a single metaphor, it somehow magically forges a stronger community. For students, it adds a concrete layer that gives them access to very abstract concepts in their learning. For teachers, it's an anchor they can all hold on to when talking about their own professional learning in a very personal way. For parents, it's a window into their children's learning at school. Carefully thought-out metaphors can transform crowds of students, teachers, and parents into learning communities.

What Is a Learning Theme?

A learning theme can be used to parallel learning in a school community for both children and adults. It captures one or more images in a short phrase or sentence, but the essence of a learning theme goes beyond being just a catchy slogan. (Although it helps if it's catchy!) A learning theme embraces learning in the classroom, can help students learn important lessons about character and friendship, and can even provide a framework for professional development. Let's take a look at how this might work.

Over the years, our school has piloted a range of learning themes. Here are some quick descriptions of a few of our favorites.

Reflect on who you are . . . be all that you can be! Adorn the school with mirrors, and introduce the idea of looking at yourself in a mirror, recognizing who you are. Then make plans for how you can continue to make yourself better and better at it all!

Take a journey in your learning and see how much you grow. Just as characters in books change as they move from place to place, treat this year as a journey in our learning. Think about how you're changing and growing through all you're doing in school.

When you think your puzzle's finished, there's always one piece left. Like a leftover piece in a jigsaw puzzle, there's always more to learn even when you think you're done. We're never really done learning, because there's always more to do.

Cross a bridge to new ideas. Build a bridge to connect ideas. When we cross bridges, we find connections that make our learning authentic. When a new idea or a new friend seems too distant for us to connect with, we find ways to build bridges to them.

See the world with fresh new eyes. Discover things unrealized! Take a look at things you thought you knew, trying to gain new understandings of them. It will help you revise your perception of the world and help you empathize with others.

Stretch, stretch, stretch, and grow. Tower taller than you'll ever know. When we challenge ourselves, we begin to outgrow ourselves. However, we can only grow taller when we overcome the initial stretch, which can be a scary thing to do.

Want something great? Create! We can create new worlds of learning around us in many ways. When we engage in that type of learning work, we re-create ourselves and our community of learning.

Study problems way up close, and see the gems inside. If you're presented with a problem with learning or with friends, try to find the good that comes from figuring out the solution.

Choosing a Theme

The previous themes didn't come from a kit of any kind. They were born from conversing, observing, and witnessing moments of growth in our learning community. Although it might be tempting to think of a clever metaphor first and retrofit a reason to it later, powerful learning themes begin with an understanding of what your school needs. Then, you can decide on the metaphor or image, and phrasing of the theme.

Think of something that puzzles you that you would like to tackle. This might be an academic or social need within the school, related to students, teachers, or parents. Think back on interactions you've had over the last year, commonalities within observations, innocent comments that might otherwise fly by you, and ask yourself what these say about your school. In the following sections, you'll find tools for developing themes from a variety of angles—addressing needs, building on strengths, and embracing new theories.

Themes That Address Needs

There might be a pattern you see in your school, almost like a recurring character flaw. Perhaps it's even causing more obvious issues, such as discipline problems. For example, one year I noticed that students and their parents had difficulty empathizing with others, and that led us to the theme of seeing the world through the eyes of others. Looking at things again had a natural academic connection to close reading, revision, and reflection. (See Figure 5.1.)

Themes That Build on Strengths

You don't have to start from a weakness. You can also build on something that you're proud of in your school. Use the same thought pattern that you used to address needs to develop your strengths-based learning theme. (See Figure 5.2.)

FIGURE 5.1

SAMPLE THEMES THAT ADDRESS NEEDS

Learning Issue (Can be about academics or character, students or teachers)	Connected Image	Related Learning (Build character off of academic, academic off of character)	Theme Title (A short, memorable phrase that captures a learning statement)
Your teachers or students need support in collaboration. (Character)	A team Joined hands	Working together in professional learning communities, small groups, using team-based games (Academic)	Teaming up for greatness! Join hands, be strong. Be together, belong!
Your students don't spend enough time reading. (Academic)	Pages in a book A clock	Caring about your work, making the most of every moment (Character)	Practice the art of using your heart! Tick-tock! Make every second count!

FIGURE 5.2

SAMPLE THEMES THAT BUILD ON STRENGTHS

Learning Strength (Can be about academics or character, students or teachers)	Connected Image	Related Learning (Build character off of academic, academic off of character)	Theme Text (A short, memorable phrase that captures a learning statement)
Your school is the model of community outreach. (Character)	A wrapped present Sharing	Sharing and celebrating our work, teaching one another (Academic)	Care enough to share! Be a teacher and a learner! Give from your heart. Give from your mind. A caring learner is the best kind!
Your school has had sustained success in writing workshop. (Academic)	A quill pen A storybook A listening ear	Listening to others tell their story. (Character)	Tell your story like it's an art. Hear someone's story with all your heart!

Themes That Help You Explore New Ideas

You might also think of a new theory in learning that you'd like to explore within your school. This can be a theory in student learning or something that you'd like your teachers to study. Use the chart in Figure 5.3 to develop your theme.

Use the chart in Figure 5.4 to consider potential learning themes for your school year.

FIGURE 5.3

SAMPLE THEMES TO EXPLORE NEW IDEAS			
Theory or Practice You'd Like to Study	**Connected Image**	**Related Learning**	**Theme Text** (A short, memorable phrase that captures a learning statement)
Growth Mindset	Growing taller Map on a journey	Not giving up	Are we there yet? We'll get there soon!
Technology Integration	A computer A robot	Find ways to make things more functional	Plug in to engineer your learning!

Pitfalls

To keep your learning theme something that supports student and professional learning, there are a few things that you might want to avoid.

Current pop culture images. Don't build your theme on the hot movie of the summer. Trends sometimes end without warning, and if the one you're considering suddenly disappears, it'll be hard to maintain momentum. Trends can also be hard to link to learning: beyond a few cute activities, they're often a dead end.

Anything that's based on only one book. Although it's always a good idea to find children's literature to support things we do in school, it's hard to sustain a theme for a whole year if it's based on one single book. If there is a book with a powerful message, try making the message

FIGURE 5.4

LEARNING THEME BRAINSTORM

Learning Issue	Connected Image	Related Learning (Build character learning off academic learning, or vice versa)	Theme Text (A short, memorable phrase that captures a learning statement)

Learning Strength	Connected Image	Related Learning (Build character learning off academic learning, or vice versa)	Theme Text (A short, memorable phrase that captures a learning statement)

Theory or Practice You'd Like to Study	Connected Image	Related Learning (Build character learning off academic learning, or vice versa)	Theme Text (A short, memorable phrase that captures a learning statement)

or theme and using the book as a supporting resource, not the star of the show. Focusing on the message rather than a particular title might also lead to other books that fit the theme.

Clichés. It's true that you can't tell a book by its cover and that it's always darkest before the dawn. However, when there's already a lot of existing schema about a cliché, it can take away people's openness about exploring it and growing new ideas together.

Cute projects. As mentioned earlier in this chapter, we can build communities around learning when it's treated as one big project, not a series of projects. When thinking about the creation of our theme, don't think in terms of activities that may seem fun on their own, but of metaphors that relate to learning as a whole.

Launching Your Learning Theme

You've decided on a theme. It's time to start thinking about how to build community and excitement around the theme. Following are some steps to get the school community thinking about the theme before the year even begins.

End-of-year faculty meeting. Share next year's learning theme with teachers in the last faculty meeting of the year. Share your ideas about ways the theme might come to life, and ask teachers to brainstorm their own ideas. It's helpful to structure this by having teachers think of ways the theme can fit into their already existing instruction, into character education, and into fun things they might have the students do. You can also think about what the timeline of the year will be. Will the school be moving toward an end-of-the-year goal? What will teachers do to keep the momentum going throughout the year? Ask them what materials they might need to do this.

Summer letter. During the summer, send a theme letter to your students. I like to start with a story about something I'm doing this summer that sneaks the metaphor into their thinking. Figure 5.5 shows a letter I used a few years ago to launch the theme of bridges. Most of my summer letters follow a similar format.

FIGURE 5.5

SAMPLE SUMMER LETTER

August 2013

Dear Boys and Girls,

A few weeks ago, my family and I went to visit Niagara Falls. This is the largest waterfall in the world. We got on a boat and wore special raincoats they gave us, even though the sun was shining. About 300 people got on this boat that went right under the fall, and we got so wet, just from the mist of the water! Everyone screamed just like on a roller coaster at the amusement park.

I start by telling the story of something I did over the summer, which leads into the theme's central metaphor.

When the boat turned around and headed back to the dock, there was a bridge above us. It's called the Rainbow Bridge, and it's one of the bridges that connect the United States with Canada. There were lots of cars on the bridge going either way, filled with Americans wanting to see Canada, and Canadians wanting to see the United States. Without that bridge and the others right by it, we'd be separated from our northern neighbors!

Looking at that bridge made me think about school. You see, when you learn things in school, you connect ideas. When you learn in school, you build bridges between yourself and the world. When you learn with friends, you connect with them in a way you just can't connect playing sports, eating and drinking, or going on a trip. When you learn together with someone, you're joined with that person by a whole different kind of friendship.

In the middle of the letter, I bring the focus back to how the experience reminds me of our school. Think about the image you have in mind for your theme, and connect it to how people learn in your school.

continues

SAMPLE SUMMER LETTER, *cont.*

At the end of the letter, I invite the students back for the first day of school. This part of the letter always reminds me of an invitation to a themed birthday party. I ask them to bring something related to the theme.

In a few short weeks, you'll be coming back to school. Your teachers and I are already preparing lots of great things for you so that you can build bridges with the world and with each other. Bring stories of your summer to share with all of us. Bring new ideas you've had about things around you. Bring in any great books you'd like to share. *Bring any pictures of you or your family on bridges during your travels.*

As my family and I headed underneath the Rainbow Bridge that day, we gasped at the same moment, because of the surprise that met us there: under the Rainbow Bridge was an actual *rainbow!* It was beautiful, and it was surprising. That's what learning can also be—beautiful, surprising, and exciting when you discover it. It's going to be a great year together! We can't wait to see you in a few short weeks!

Yours in learning,

Mr. Marshall

Launching assembly. Bringing the whole school together gets everyone excited about the new learning theme. Figure 5.6 shows the plan for the launching assembly we used for the learning theme "Stretch, stretch, stretch and grow . . . Tower taller than you'll ever know." You can use a similar structure for your own launching assemblies.

FIGURE 5.6

SAMPLE LAUNCHING ASSEMBLY STRUCTURE

Activity	Time Frame	Example	What This Activity Accomplishes
Welcome	2 minutes	The principal welcomes everyone and tells them that our learning will be exciting.	Creates anticipation for today and what's to come during the course of the year
Whole-group activity for students	5 minutes	The physical education teacher invites students to stretch their legs so it's comfortable, and then to stretch until their legs start tingling, and then to stretch until they eventually experience slight discomfort. The teacher explains that that tingling and slight pain signal that new muscles are starting to develop. The principal ties this to learning, saying that when we feel confused or frustrated by challenges, new learning starts to happen in our minds.	Gives students an experience that relates to the learning theme's central metaphor
Small-group activity for students	10 minutes	In small groups, teachers show a resistance band and measure its length. The students take turns stretching it slightly and remeasuring it each time. They talk about how each time it stretches, it grows.	Gives students opportunities to interact and experience the learning together

continues

SAMPLE LAUNCHING ASSEMBLY STRUCTURE, *cont.*			
Activity	**Time Frame**	**Example**	**What This Activity Accomplishes**
Framing goals within the theme	5 minutes	A teacher shares a slide show with famous towers and buildings, talking about their height, comparing the height of each edifice to the height of a person, a house, their school. The teacher begins transferring out of the idea of stretching into the idea of towers that are much, much taller than we are.	Helps students to see how the learning theme includes goals for growth
Individual goal setting and goal tracking	7 minutes	The principal reveals a shoe box that has been decorated and has the word *cornerstone* on it with the date. The principal explains that this year, school members are going to stretch and challenge themselves so that they can build a huge tower of learning. Each student places an index card with a previously written goal into the box. Each month, all classes will add a brick to the tower stating the students' learning on top of their goals in the cornerstone. The box will be sealed and opened again at the end of the year like a time capsule, and everyone will have the chance to reread their goal at the end of the year.	Builds anticipation for the learning that will occur this year and gives students a tangible way to measure their goals and growth across the year

Sustaining Your Theme Throughout the Year with Students

The beginning of the year is replete with enthusiasm for the work and the memories that are on their way. However, as the months roll by, the learning theme can fall by the wayside. This sin of omission can lead us to forget to build community as we turn the pages of the calendar. Throughout the year, we can sustain the energy associated with the launch of the new year.

Figure out a tool for regular reflection, and use it! On long road trips, we can reenergize by looking at a map each time we make a stop and mark just how far we've come, noting that we only have so much left to travel. During the school year, we can provide moments to reflect (even with our youngest students), tying these reflective moments to the learning theme in some way.

Create a centrally located display where students can add their reflections regularly. For example, when we used the puzzle theme in our school, students built a life-size jigsaw puzzle and each class added a monthly reflection to a large puzzle piece. During our tower theme, each class added a decorated shoebox with monthly reflections inside to build a tower at the front of the school. We used milestone dates for adding new reflections. As students see the creation growing slowly, they begin to see their own growth as well.

Engage students in opportunities to reflect on their individual work, in writing or orally. For example, during our journey theme, each student created a passport, which they "stamped" with a regular reflection on how they've grown. Another option is for teachers to ask their students to tell the story of how they've grown in the last few weeks and to set goals for themselves.

Gather students together to talk about their learning. When our school's theme focused on creating, the entire school gathered for thirty minutes every three weeks for a school share, during which classes or individual students would show something they had learned. During our bridge theme, classes paired up for a special activity each month to do something fun that somehow tied in to their learning. During one of these "bridging" gatherings, first graders and third graders, who had both just finished a unit of study on nonfiction writing, shared their published pieces with one another. Another session brought two fourth-grade classes together to share math games they had created around division. Yet another pairing allowed two classes that had just finished a study of the solar system to play *Space Jeopardy!,* a game created by their teachers. These gatherings are powerful for students: they get to see and hear each other talking with pride about what they've worked on. This also gives teachers a way to talk and learn from each other.

Circulate theme kits around the school to jump-start reflective conversation. When our school's theme was about journeys, kits were backpacks, suitcases, and other packages, filled with travel-based read-alouds, quotes about journeys and changing, and a vehicle toy. When our theme was related to vision, we circulated kits with vision artifacts, which set up parallels between the objects (a microscope enlarges tiny things so you can study them up close) and learning (looking at the details of something to figure it out). We set dates when the kits would be passed from room to room, and the teachers talked through the contents with their students. Kits require more planning over the summer, but they are easy to implement through the year once the prep work is done, and they help to reignite the community's interest in the themes.

Create a regular newsletter that relates to your theme. Write and distribute a newsletter for students that begins with a section about the learning theme. Using a structure like the one shown in Figure 5.7 helps me to relate the theme to social or academic learning.

Involve families. Another way to build community and momentum is to involve families in your learning theme during the year.

- Reference the theme consistently in communications with parents—in newsletters, in blog posts, and in the school's social media accounts.

- Ask families to send in artifacts related to your theme—photos of kids in front of *bridges,* for example, or a collection of items that kids use to *create*—explaining why you're asking for it and how you'll be using it. We've seen fun discussions among parents on social media relating to these requests.

- If your school has a parent organization, the members may be interested in fund-raising for special assemblies or other project-related materials.

FIGURE 5.7

Cross a bridge to new ideas . . . Build a bridge to connect them

The Bridge

A newsletter for Stoney Lane

Dear Boys and Girls!

This is the Akashi-Kaikyo Bridge found in Kobe-Naruto, Japan. It measures 1,991 meters (over one mile!) in length, making it the longest suspension bridge. Built in 1998, this bridge's name actually translates to "Pearl Bridge"!

> *Begin with some fun information that's related to the learning theme. The year that our school's theme focused on bridges, each newsletter began with a profile of a different bridge.*

Do you know how pearls are formed? Deep under the ocean, oysters live a very calm sort of life. No one bothers them. They just sit there. However, every once in a while, a piece of sand slips inside its hard shell. This bothers the oyster, irritating it by picking away at it. In order to protect itself from this irritation, the oyster puts a coat of special material around the sand so that it doesn't bother it any more. The sand soon has a shiny coating, and that's called a pearl. Imagine that! Something so beautiful starting off as an irritation!

This happens to so many of us, too. Sometimes, there are things in our lives that irritate us. Brothers and sisters. Extra homework. Rules we just don't like. Rain on a Saturday. Things that are hard. Wouldn't it be easier sometimes to do without these things? They're just so irritating!

> *Connect the new information or the theme to something that students can identify with academically or socially.*

However, if we let these things be and live with them for a little while, they might just turn into the pearls we never expected them to be. Brothers and sisters grow up and become our good friends. Extra homework can make you smarter. We learn that rules keep us safe. Saturday rain can make us remember a favorite board game we forgot. Challenges make us stronger.

> *Show how the theme can help students to learn and grow, and invite them to join in.*

So remember the lesson of this wise bridge! Next time something bothers you, don't cry out, "It's not fair!" Wait around and see what beautiful pearl might be on its way into your life!

Sustaining Your Theme Throughout the Year with Teachers

The learning theme can create excitement about learning for your students and build community among them. It can do the same for your teachers as well. Roland Barth (1990), author and founder of the Harvard Principal's Center, tells us how critical it is in the life of a school to have teachers who live as learners, supporting and nourishing one another in collegial relationships. Learning themes can help teachers by providing a sense of community, a common mission, and a clear idea of how their work contributes to the overall theme. Here are some ways to use your learning theme with your staff.

Allow the learning theme to influence your word choice. For example, when discussing next steps with teachers in response to their observations and evaluations, integrate the metaphor your school has adopted during the year. Figure 5.8 offers some examples of what this might look like in conversations.

Integrate the theme into faculty meetings and professional development. Learning themes can help us approach professional learning in a positive way, focusing on the rich possibilities ahead rather than on perceived deficits.

In the professional learning band of your faculty meeting, refer to your theme. If the topic you're discussing has an obvious correlation to your theme, go with it. If the connection is more metaphorical, perhaps use it to title that section of the meeting. Don't feel compelled to constrain meetings to only those topics that directly connect to the theme.

When talking through something the teachers are learning, use the language of the theme to help you keep the talk positive. For example, instead of saying, "Some of us have really been struggling with conferring," use the metaphor of the theme to help you all focus on the possibilities that the future holds, such as, "This year we're going to *take a journey* in our understandings of conferring," "We're going to *stretch what we know* about conferring now," or "We're going to *look* at conferring *differently.*"

LEARNING THEME LANGUAGE EXAMPLES

FIGURE 5.8

Question to Prompt Teacher Reflection	Learning Theme Journeys	Learning Theme Bridges	Learning Theme Looking with Fresh Eyes
What's your biggest professional goal for this year?	What's the next step in your journey as a teacher?	How will you build a bridge this year to the teacher you want to be?	What do you hope to see in a new way this year?
What was your biggest realization from this observation?	How did the journey of this lesson change you as a teacher?	What bridge did you cross in this lesson?	What do you see differently than you did before this lesson?
How did you grow the most this past year?	Where have you arrived at the end of the journey of this year?	What new connections did this year bring you?	How do you see yourself differently as a teacher than you did before?

Celebrating the Theme at the End of the Year

The final celebration of a learning theme solidifies what's been learned and bonds the community together in a feeling of success. Although there is no one recipe for how to have a celebration, here are a few ideas that might be important to keep it about learning.

Everyone should bring something. Students and teachers should bring something, whether it's a written reflection or a symbol, that ties to the metaphor of the year. Then, during the celebration, everyone should have an opportunity to put this item to use. In the story at the beginning of this chapter, for example, students used their rocks to make a rainbow display. When our school's theme was about *vision*, each student brought a piece to contribute to a mosaic. Contributing a physical object to the cause helps everyone feel a little bit of ownership in the event. Take a look at the eye mosaic in Figure 5.9. Each little piece is a student reflection.

If you've been building something, be sure it's there. If you've built a tower or created a mural or devised some other physical manifestation of the year's ongoing work, be sure to have it be there at your celebration. This object has helped students and teachers gauge their growth all year. It ought to be at your celebration.

Involve symbolism and imagery. Make sure that there is some visual representation of the theme. If students have a hand in making it, even better!

Do something hands-on. During the celebration, engage students in doing something: talking, building, creating, solving a problem. Ideally, the learning they've done all year has been active. The culmination of the learning should be that way, too!

Share multiple voices. This is not your show. Be sure you allow students and teachers to have a visible role in the celebration by teaching something, by sharing their learning, or by facilitating an activity.

Keep it about learning and reflection. Although it's nice to have juice or some treats, too much emphasis on snacks or trinkets will be a distraction. Let the learning be the star of the show.

Make the celebration brief. At our school, we aim for about thirty to forty-five minutes for this event. If the event feels too long to kids, excitement will dissipate. Don't let the event last long enough to feel boring.

The Final Stretch!

In this chapter, we've discussed how you can choose a learning theme and help it take root for the benefit of your students, your staff, and your students' families. We've seen how learning themes can unite school communities, which

FIGURE 5.9

OUR LEARNING THEME MOSAIC, MADE UP OF STUDENT REFLECTIONS

is a help to you as a leader. I'd like to end this chapter by including an example of how learning themes can help the principal as a learner, as well.

Our learning theme one year was, "Stretch, stretch, stretch and grow . . . Tower taller than you'll ever know!" It was a study of stretching ourselves with challenges and outgrowing ourselves by learning newer and newer things. We studied famous towers and strived to grow taller and taller in our learning. That December, my school year was interrupted by an accident. While hanging Christmas lights, the ladder slipped out from under me, and I fell, breaking both of my arms, in two places each.

Some major surgery was followed by lots of therapy to help me gain back my strength and range of motion. For four months, I was home working on my newest project: healing. In between therapy sessions, my own home exercises, and watching reruns on TV, I kept up with writing my newsletter for the students, helping them learn important life lessons by learning about famous towers around the world. I wanted my arms to be as they were, but healing was such hard work. Days turned to weeks. Weeks turned to months. When would this be over? When could I go back to work? When could I pick up my kids? When could I even bend my arms enough touch my face?

One afternoon, my cell phone buzzed—someone had sent me pictures. The students had created their own towers out of materials they brought in from home. Each tower was accompanied by brief explanations of what each one was and what it represented for each child's progress. I felt the satisfaction of seeing the work I'd nurtured going on even without me, because I'd helped bring others to it. It was also a reminder that this work of stretching beyond one's comfort zone was not just for the students and the staff—it was also for me.

Seeing the students' progress gave me new energy to push on in my own healing. A few months later, at our year-end celebration, I told the students about the stretching I had to do to heal, and how sometimes, it hurt. I told them that whenever it was tough, I thought of them, stretching themselves beyond what was easy, into newer challenges. Then, extending my arm high and straight, a goal I'd worked months to reach, I told them honestly, "Look at what I can do now, because of you. You gave me so much this year."

Chapter 6

NURTURE THE LEARNER WITHIN

My son Kende was born with bilateral club feet. He was casted from the time he was four days old. He wore special shoes with braces on them. Things looked promising, but when he was four-and-a-half, the condition began to recur. We had no choice but surgery.

A week before he turned five, Kende underwent surgery to correct the problem. Part of the corrective process was that he needed to be casted up to his thighs with his knees bent. Tears filled his eyes as he realized this meant he wouldn't be able to walk and that he needed to be in a wheelchair temporarily.

One day, I came home from work, and he greeted me at the door. "How did you do that?" I asked him. "Check this out," he said, and he stood up, knees bent, torso leaning forward, hands clasped on furniture, and maneuvered his way around the room. He had taught himself to use the strength in his arms to move around.

He was so motivated, wanting to walk so much that during this nine-week period he taught himself five different ways to get around the house! Kende was mobile, and when his casts finally came off, there was a new air of confidence to this five-year-old, who walked a little bit taller because he wouldn't let anything get him down!

I share this story because Kende's persistence points to the question at the heart of this book: Why do we learn? Children and adults, students of school, and students of life learn with greatest investment when they are engaged in what they are doing, when they feel that their learning is meaningful and relevant. Brian Cambourne (1995) identifies engagement as one of his conditions of learning. He tells us that engagement occurs when learners are convinced of the following:

- They are potential doers.
- Engaging with what they are learning will further the purposes of their lives.
- They can engage and try to emulate without fear of physical or psychological hurt if their attempts are not fully correct.

These conditions were all a part of Kende's journey back to mobility. They motivated him to be successful. His desire to be able to get around the house and the world outside raised his sense of curiosity and investment.

So you, the head learner, have thought about supporting student learning, teacher learning, and bringing learning to colleagues in groups. You've thought about finding connections between learning and the many management decisions you must make. Now it's time to focus inward, on the learning that's happening within you. Without that, you'll quickly become the principal you don't want to be—bogged down in the administration of someone else's vision, the disciplinarian and scheduler, the enforcer of the contracts and the mandates, the building manager. You'll lose the drive that moved Kende back to mobility and the rewards of the learning cycle that made you want to be a teacher in the first place. How do we nurture the learner within ourselves to keep the magic going?

One of the factors that brings excitement and engagement to learning is finding something that fills a void. In the introduction to this book, we talked about losing something when we gain something. This can be spun positively, also. When you learn something, you lose the void that had existed in your life, whether you knew it was there or not.

If we were doctors, we'd be in the business of health, and therefore be compelled and strive to live a healthy lifestyle. Teachers and principals are in the business of learning. How credible are we if we ourselves don't live a life of learning, even once we're in the principal's office? It's one of the most essential parts of our work, isn't it? Here are some ways to invite new learning into your life professionally.

Listen and Start a Trail of Thought

I remember sitting in a keynote given by Christopher Lehman, my friend and former colleague from the Teachers College Reading and Writing Project. He was talking about innovation and the steps some schools were taking to foster innovation. He told stories and shared pictures of something called *makerspaces*, and I just remember thinking that it was cool. As I took notes, I started wondering about how I could make this fit the finite confines of my own school. How could I make this work? My trail of thinking was sort of like the classic picture book, *If You Give a Mouse a Cookie,* by Laura Numeroff (1985). The trail was, "If *A*, then *B*. If *B*, then *C*. If *C*, then *D*."

> *If* I started using makerspaces, *then* it might spark more creativity and innovation in my students and my teachers.

> *If* my students and my teachers became more creative and innovative, *then* they might take what they know to newer and newer levels, without giving up, and add new ideas to our school.

> *If* they worked harder without giving up and added new ideas to our school, *then* it might add to the excitement of our overall learning community.

The conclusion I reach could result in making my school community (or even my district or beyond) a much richer learning environment. This is important, but the bonus is that if we decide to work on this idea together, I'm learning alongside them, participating in the wondering, the immersion, the approximation, the practice, and the feedback. It's exciting for me, because it's adding a new layer to my own learning. It's exciting for my teachers and my students, because they see me learning with them in this enthusiastic and yes, possibly vulnerable, role.

There are also lots of ministeps to get from *A* to *B*. It's easy to think that we have to follow the exact steps we've seen used elsewhere to be successful. This isn't the case. For example, sometimes visitors come to our school to see how we're using workshop teaching. Rather than looking for possibilities for their own schools, they focus on how they can't do workshop because of the differences between our schools because we're in a suburban setting, for example, or because some of our rooms are bigger, or some of our class sizes are a bit smaller. They write off the possibility of success without considering what they might do differently and what strengths they can capitalize on in their own schools. Instead, we have to imagine how we can make the vision work in our own real worlds. Here's what my thinking looked like as I looked at makerspaces in another school and considered how we might use makerspaces in my school (see Figure 6.1).

When we start thinking about possibilities, it excites the learner inside us. We can begin to imagine directions to take in our schools and ourselves.

Read Professionally . . . a Lot!

Matt Renwick (2017), a Wisconsin elementary school principal and author, writes about the need for principals to engage in daily professional reading that relates to their own learning goals and the goals of their school. He writes that he used to feel like he should hide the fact that he was reading professionally on the job, but he came to realize that it's not something that should

FIGURE 6.1

IMAGINING SOLUTIONS TO POSSIBLE ROADBLOCKS

I'm seeing or hearing that . . .	But, this might be a problem because . . .	So, maybe . . .
This school uses their hallways to house makerspaces.	I don't have much hallway space available.	I can use common areas like the library or art room, or something simpler in every classroom.
This school has invested in a lot of engineering equipment.	My teachers and I don't even know how to use this equipment.	I can start with simpler materials like blocks and household items. We can also read up on it.
This initiative is led by the school's science lab teacher.	I don't have a science lab teacher.	I can start a study group with interested teachers who can lead the charge.

be hidden. As the principal of the school, it's his *job* to be up on his game, and it's good for others to know he is! It's like working out at the gym and seeing the trainers working out alongside you. You know they take their work very seriously. Now for the next step: figuring out what to read. There is so much literature out there for educators. How do you figure out just what to read?

Social Media

Recently, most of my professional reading diet comes from what I read on Twitter, where people share not only pithy tweets but also links to a wide array of information. I only use my Twitter account for professional purposes, and even then, it can be an overwhelming task to keep up with everything that comes through on my feed. It's important to decide which voices to listen to. Figure 6.2 shows the formula I've been using to decide about who to follow carefully on social media.

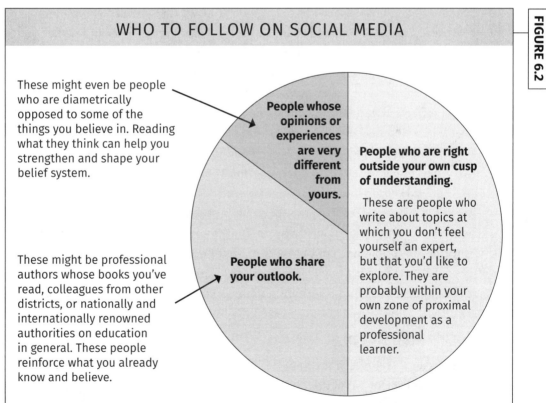

FIGURE 6.2

WHO TO FOLLOW ON SOCIAL MEDIA

These might even be people who are diametrically opposed to some of the things you believe in. Reading what they think can help you strengthen and shape your belief system.

People whose opinions or experiences are very different from yours.

People who are right outside your own cusp of understanding.

These are people who write about topics at which you don't feel yourself an expert, but that you'd like to explore. They are probably within your own zone of proximal development as a professional learner.

These might be professional authors whose books you've read, colleagues from other districts, or nationally and internationally renowned authorities on education in general. These people reinforce what you already know and believe.

People who share your outlook.

My examples are taken from Twitter, because that's where the bulk of my own professional reading on social media occurs. Although Twitter may not be your social media of choice (or may seem dated if you're reading this book years from now), the same principles can help you consider where you might want to look for new ideas in your reading.

Professional Books

Did you ever feel like the food or drink you once loved has become somehow less than your favorite? Did you hate vegetables as a kid and then grow to love them? Scientists tell us that as we grow older, our taste buds and our brains cause us to change our tastes. Professional tastes and interests change, as well. I remember reading everything I could possibly find about the teaching of writing. Then I went through a phase where I owned every book on the teaching of spelling and grammar. Then for a few more years, I found myself reading more about teaching in a balanced literacy model. Today, I find myself reading more and more about learning leadership and more general theories about learning. Why does this happen? Do we have professional taste buds that evolve with us?

Yes and no. Although there aren't real physical nodules on our bodies that control what we like to read, our lives and interests control our tastes, of course. However, researchers dating back to Louise Rosenblatt and her transactional theory (1978) tell us about the interaction of the reader and the text: where we are in our lives and the goals that occupy our time and attention help determine what we choose to read, and how we think about it.

Set aside some money and treat yourself to a professional text shopping spree twice a year. Get to know the publishers who put out books that deal with the topics that are your flavor du jour, so to speak. Find out when your three or four publishers put out most of their books, mark your calendar, and go online to see what's new. If you receive hard copies of their catalogs, go through them and choose a handful of books you'll be able to read and apply.

Journal Articles

In Chapter 1, we studied the importance of networking with colleagues across schools and across the nation. Joining professional organizations whose missions match your professional goal opens up a great many opportunities to feed your own learning. Three of my favorites—Association for Supervision and Curriculum Development, National Council of Teachers of English, and International Literacy Association—each have journals to which I subscribe. Subscribing to journals will help to ensure there is always something on your "to be read" pile. Imagine the example you'll create for your teachers and students by having such a pile on your desk when they come to talk to you in your office.

Half the fun of finding good professional texts and reading them is sharing them with others. In our school, each Friday, I share one article with my teachers that I think will interest them. The articles usually have something to do with what's new in the field, or a topic we're unpacking as a group. Sometimes, they're just there to inspire. What do we do with these articles? *Nothing.* There's no formal discussion. I don't ask for a reflection, or a retell, or a diorama, or anything. Part of the reason is that I don't want them to feel like I'm adding one more thing to their plate, or that I'm expecting that it be read by a certain time. By just inviting them to do this reading and not holding them to the article, I find that teachers are *more engaged* in diving in. I see it in observations. I hear it in conversation. I feel it as I walk around. The best part is that this helps feed me as a learner! It's like sharing a favorite recipe and feeling the satisfaction of smelling its aroma when I visit.

Read Widely, and Read the World Around You

If we expect our students to read for pleasure, we have to do this also. Yes, read your junk! This could be fiction in any genre, or nonfiction about any favorite topic. I don't really consider myself a fiction reader, but the two topics I find myself reading the most in nonfiction are presidential history and classic TV. I'm not sure how these two topics fit together. I find that when I read these for pleasure, I start growing new ideas about my life. Figure 6.3 are some examples from my reading in presidential history.

When I was a kid, I found it fascinating that William Howard Taft was so overweight that he needed a special bathtub in the White House and that Dolly Madison served oyster-flavored ice cream at White House gatherings.

FIGURE 6.3

LET YOUR OWN READING INFLUENCE YOUR WORK
(My own reading about presidential history . . .)

Something I Read	What That Makes Me Think
Ronald Reagan delegated a great deal of his power to those who worked under him. George W. Bush was a chronic micromanager.	Which style of leadership sounds more like me?
John Adams and Thomas Jefferson had an on-again, off-again "bromance" where they were very close, and then wouldn't speak for years and years.	That's a very complex relationship. Does that remind me of anyone in my professional life? In my personal life?
John F. Kennedy is remembered as being courageous for taking responsibility for the Bay of Pigs Invasion, acknowledging it was a mistake.	How do I handle my errors as a leader? How does this affect those under my care?

These are trivial facts that are interesting. Now, however, as an adult in the position I'm in, I try to relate to what I read and let it affect me. It's true that this might seem easier to connect through the lens of presidential history. It's about leadership. But can *anything* I'm interested in truly help me in my professional growth? Let's look at something where the lens is less apparent: classic TV (see Figure 6.4).

You can also read the world around you differently if you think about your work within it. As I mentioned earlier, about a year ago, I broke both of my arms when I fell off a ladder. The long recovery process involved surgery and a great deal of occupational therapy. Just going through this process deepened my understanding of what learning really is. Observe your surroundings, and let them lead you to new ideas about the work of learning and leadership (see Figure 6.5).

The healing process helped me deepen my own thinking about the practices my teachers and I engage in for real learning to happen.

LET YOUR OWN READING INFLUENCE YOUR WORK
(My own reading about classic TV . . .)

FIGURE 6.4

Something I Read	What That Makes Me Think
There was a lot of feuding on the set of *Three's Company*, because of contractual issues.	What kind of relationships do I have with my colleagues? My family? What role does money play?
Although it started out as a show kids could enjoy, *Bewitched* eventually became a platform for social issues like discrimination and diverse families.	What is the underlying power of what I do? What will be my legacy as a school leader? As a person?
Although she could have called her boss, "Lou," Mary Richards on *The Mary Tyler Moore Show* chose to call him "Mr. Grant."	Why would someone choose to humble herself in this work relationship? How did it affect them? Does that happen in our school?

LET YOUR OWN EXPERIENCES INFLUENCE YOUR WORK
(My own experiences with occupational therapy . . .)

FIGURE 6.5

Observation	Reflection
The activities I took on at occupational therapy were often game based.	There is power to learning and practicing through play.
The therapists took a mix of quantitative and qualitative notes.	This is like the data we collect through reading logs and conferring notes.
When my range of motion plateaued, I had to wear splints for a few hours each day.	When we get stuck, we need more intense interventions.
The goals and many home activities were about real-life skills.	Context is important to growth.
Therapists would start with what I was doing well, and then push me with small goals.	There is a balance of complimenting and teaching within a zone of proximal development.

Write to Spark Ideas and Learning

Our jobs are full of interruptions, urgent situations, and decisions that affect many other people. After a day of dealing with late busses, worried parents, or concerned teachers, we may wonder where visionary principals get so many good ideas, when all we can manage is to hold things down as best we can. Are other principals gifted with extra energy? Flashes of inspiration? Great luck? Maybe. However, I think it's more likely that they've developed a habit of cultivating ideas.

One of the greatest gifts to children's education is the writer's notebook: a notebook that writers keep to gather their thinking—their observations—in a very informal way. We might think of a writer's notebook as a kind of shoebox in which we gather things we find in our lives. Some of what we gather may eventually be useful in writing something else, something more polished: a published poem, some nonfiction writing, an essay, a letter that you'll send to someone in hopes of making a change. Some of what we gather may never be "useful" in that regard, but the act of gathering helps us to notice the world around us. In his evergreen text, *The Writer's Notebook,* Ralph Fletcher also explains what a writer's notebook is *not*: "A writer's notebook is not a diary: 'Today it is raining. We have a substitute teacher named Miss Pampanella. She seems very nice. We are going to have gym right before lunch.' It's not a reading journal in which your teacher tells you to summarize the main idea of a book, or write a letter to a character" (1996, 3). A writer's notebook belongs to the writer.

Your professional writer's notebook can be the place where you gather your ideas-in-waiting that can be developed into something else: a blog post, a keynote, a workshop, the long-term study of a topic with your teachers, a professional article, a chapter in a professional book.

Getting Started

If you'd like to get started, but aren't sure where, you can try on some of these strategies to start thinking reflectively and begin gathering ideas. Once you get into the habit of using your notebook, you can:

- Make a timeline of yourself as a leader (or teacher). Choose one significant (challenging, transformative, rewarding, etc.) moment from the timeline, and write long about it.

- Make a timeline of yourself as a learner. Choose one significant (successful, difficult, inspirational, etc.) moment from the timeline, and write long about it.

- Choose a student or a teacher who intrigues you, and record anecdotes of your interactions with him or her, including your own reflections.

- Choose a topic that you're studying professionally. Keep a log of that topic in action in your school.

- Think of a time in your professional life that surprised you. Write about the time, how it surprised you, and what you learned from it.

- Choose one aspect of professional practice (like observing teachers, dealing with difficult parents, etc.); write about moments throughout your career dealing with the practice, and think about how or why you've changed.

- Write an account about a teacher, then reflect. Allow your reflection to remind you of another teacher, then reflect again. Follow this chain reaction for as many steps as you'd like. Then, consider—what new conclusion might these pieces lead you toward?

Most of the previous ideas are *qualitative* in nature. However, you can also use your notebook to gather *quantitative* information. When people diet, they often write down all the foods they eat to hold themselves accountable, but also to look for patterns in their eating to make life changes. When readers read, we often ask them to write down what they're reading so that we can make teaching plans based on interests, levels, and habits. As principals, we can learn from patterns and habits in the same way. Here are some types of *quantitative* notebook entries:

- Record the number of interactions with a teacher about a topic. You might want to add a *qualitative* component by noting how the teacher's understanding of that topic has evolved.

- Record the time something takes (length of lessons, units, procedures, etc.) and look for patterns.

- Record the volume of something (number of pages, student scores, activities) and look for patterns.

- Record the instances you witness something (something on a bulletin board, a turn of phrase you hear, a level of questioning, a type of work, etc.) and look for patterns.

Reflecting Through Your Notebook

After you have about five to ten entries, you might start to go through the notebook and look for patterns. The patterns might lead you to a bigger idea that you wish to explore. Maybe you find that your writing deals with ways to support newer teachers, creating positive change in your school's culture, or balancing the leadership and management aspects of your work. If you'd like to do more with these ideas, consider using the table in Figure 6.6 to help you make plans.

From Notebooks to the World

Once you choose the audience, you can decide where and how to share your ideas. Each type of writing or sharing has its own structure that's needed.

FIGURE 6.6

IMAGINING THE AUDIENCE OR GENRE FOR YOUR OWN PROFESSIONAL WRITING		
If my topic is . . .	**A good audience might be . . .**	**And a good genre or venue for my writing might be . . .**
Something specific to the instruction within my school	The teachers in my school	A workshop (if it's technical or trainable) or keynote (if it's inspirational) A faculty meeting
Something specific to the culture of my school	The teachers in my school The parents in my school	A faculty meeting A PTA meeting
Something of general interest outside my school or district that can be captured in a small space	Colleagues in other districts	A blog post
Something of general interest outside my school or district that should be fleshed out	Colleagues in other districts	A professional article (Consider the magazine or journal best aligned with your topic.)

- The best *workshops* have takeaways that teachers can use immediately. *Keynotes* have some of that, but mostly serve to inspire. Kathy Collins, author of many books on primary reading instruction, often says she likes to give *keyshops*, which are equally inspirational and practical.

- *Blogs* tend to be brief. They have their own particular flavor or feeling, often balancing hands-on suggestions and inspiration.

- If you're writing an *article*, you'll need to expand. When deciding on which journal to write for, think about the type of writing in the journal. For example, *The Reading Teacher*, the journal of the International Literacy Association, focuses on very specific aspects of teaching reading. *Educational Leadership,* the journal of Association for Supervision and Curriculum Development features, gives each issue its own thematic focus and is written with the principal in mind.

When you go through your notebook, take a look to see what and how much information you have. Do you have confidential information about a teacher's practices that can't really be shared? Do you have very specific teaching strategies you're exploring? Are you exploring theories that are current in research that you're blending with what's going on in classrooms? These things might help you decide on how you will share your ideas.

This careful read of your notebook may also help you to see what's *not* there. For example, you might see there is a lot of good inspirational information, but you want to examine more students to test out your idea. Looking for what's *not* in your notebook can prompt you to try new avenues for learning, such as visiting classrooms, reading targeted professional literature, consulting student data, or talking to teachers. Even the process of sharing out your learning can be generative.

Teach to Learn

When you teach something, you learn it twice. Teaching something helps you understand it at a deeper level. Therefore, you can deepen your learning by making an appointment to teach something regularly. Appointment teaching is a commitment to growing your own understanding. Here's a plan for appointment teaching across the year, using the study of flow theory (Csikszentmihalyi 1990) as an example.

FIGURE 6.7

APPOINTMENT TEACHING ACROSS THE YEAR: A SAMPLE PLAN

Time Frame	Audience / Format	Content
September	Your teachers / faculty meeting	A TED Talk on flow theory and discuss its impact on our teaching
October	Your teachers / grade-level meetings	Assessing the level of engagement in students while they are reading
November	Principals in other districts / Twitter chat	Identifying engagement in teachers and students when observing them
December	Parents in your school / PTA meeting	What is flow theory? Identifying and supporting engagement in our children
January	Teachers in your district / keynote address at a professional development day	Taking a close look at engagement versus compliance in ourselves and students
February	Your teachers / faculty meeting	Looking for signs of engagement in a peer-led walk-through
March	Your teachers / grade-level meetings	Naming ways to move students along an engagement continuum
April	Principals in other districts / book club	Article share with principals in other schools and districts around the idea of engagement
May	Students in your school / classroom lesson	Identifying if you're enjoying your work, and strategizing how you'll become more engaged
June	Your teachers / faculty meeting	Reflecting on our study of engagement; setting goals for exploring it more next year

The flow theory example shows how you can grow thinking about one topic with multiple groups across a year. By teaching it to such a diverse set of audiences (students, parents, teachers, principal colleagues), you get to study it from multiple perspectives. Don't worry about feeling you need to be an expert on the topic before you start. A head learner keeps on learning alongside others. That's part of what makes the journey an exciting one.

Create Communities of Joy...for Us All

Katherine Paterson, author of many classic children's books including *The Bridge to Terabithia* (1977) and *The Great Gilly Hopkins* (1978), once addressed thousands of teachers at a gathering at Riverside Church, where she shared a study that asked hundreds of people what they remember most about elementary school. Only one mentioned an academic subject. Most of them mentioned friends, a special teacher, a humiliating event, or a moment of creativity like writing, art, or being in a play.

We can probably relate to these people, naming similar memories from our own lives. These memories are tied together by a single word: *joy*. The reason for that is simple. It's what we hope for as we, even in summer months, look forward to September and the school year that is coming. Joy is probably one of the main reasons we entered this profession to begin with—we chose this work because of our joy for kids, our joy for learning, our joy for helping kids get there. But so many factors easily take away joy from our children's lives at school. It's hard to keep our own joy going. It's true that you have to keep your eye on testing and curriculum, but first and foremost, we have to keep our eyes on the kids, working with teachers to create environments in which they can all learn. Choosing books of beauty to read or share with others, having rich conversations, and feeding our own learning lives . . . these are what will bring joy to the children in our care and the adults whose lives we touch.

It's hard to be in education nowadays. The world is watching. Parents don't always understand that we, too are acting as their children's advocates. The public often confuses their own school experiences with an understanding of the complexities of school leadership. Local and national political leaders may mistakenly believe that they can always quantify our work, the craft of teaching and learning, and even students' successes and potential from afar.

However, we can make the most of what we do have control of. We have control of the choices we make each day when we work with kids. We can decide that we will make time to learn and to create systems in which both our teachers and our students learn. We can implement professional knowledge in our education, thanks to the work of giants in our field who have come before us, many of whom are still actively helping kids, teachers, and leaders like us. We can draw strength from our colleagues across the hall and across the country, with whom we share ideas. We have the control to establish local communities of learning, so that we feel less alone. We can create communities—groups of people united by a common goal, a goal that fortifies them and pushes them ahead to do their best work.

It is up to us to make school the place we want for our *children*—the joyful place where they can learn, grow, explore, and trust that their best efforts will be met with adults' best efforts to help them succeed. It is up to us to make school the place we want for our *teachers*—the joyful place where they feel safe and confident enough to treat their students with care, the place where they feel secure and supported enough to take risks for the sake of children's learning and well-being. It is up to us to make school the place we want for *ourselves*—where we can serve in the best interest of others, making decisions that will help them build the future, while we ourselves find fulfillment in our work, satisfied that we have not given up, but nurtured and passed on the tradition of learning and teaching as it has stood for hundreds of years.

References

Abdul-Jabbar, Kareem. 2017. *Coach Wooden and Me: Our 50-Year Friendship On and Off the Court.* New York: Grand Central Publishing.

Allen, Jennifer. 2006. *Becoming a Literacy Leader: Supporting Learning and Change.* Portland, ME: Stenhouse.

Allington, Richard L. 2001. *What Really Matters for Struggling Readers: Designing Research-Based Programs.* Upper Saddle River, NJ: Pearson Education.

Anderson, Carl. 2000. *How's It Going? A Practical Guide to Conferring with Student Writers.* Portsmouth, NH: Heinemann.

Barth, Roland. 1990. *Improving Schools from Within: Teachers, Parents, and Principals Can Make the Difference.* San Francisco: Jossey-Bass.

———. 1997. *The Principal Learner: A Work in Progress.* Cambridge: International Network of Principals' Centers, Harvard Graduate School of Education.

———. 2001. *Learning By Heart.* San Francisco: Jossey-Bass.

———. 2007. The Jossey-Bass Reader on Educational Leadership, 2nd Ed. Edited by Michael Fullan. Sanfrancisco: Wiley.

Beers, G. Kylene., and Robert E. Probst. 2013. *Notice & Note: Strategies for Close Reading.* Portsmouth, NH: Heinemann.

Calkins, Lucy. 2001. *The Art of Teaching Reading.* Portsmouth, NH: Heinemann.

Calkins, Lucy, and Laurie Pessah. 2008. *A Principal's Guide to Leadership in the Teaching of Writing: Professional Development in the Teaching of Writing; Helping Teachers with Units of Study.* Portsmouth, NH: Firsthand/Heinemann.

Cambourne, Brian. 1995. "Toward An Educationally Relevant Theory Of Literacy Learning: Twenty Years Of Inquiry." *The Reading Teacher* 49 (3).

City, Elizabeth A. 2014. "Talking to Learn." ASCD: *Educational Leadership* 72 (3): 10–16.

City, Elizabeth A., Richard F. Elmore, Sarah E. Fiarman, and Lee Teitel. 2014. *Instructional Rounds in Education: A Network Approach to Improving Teaching and Learning.* Cambridge, MA: Harvard Education.

Csikszentmihalyi, Mihaly. 1990. *Flow: the Psychology of Optimal Experience.* New York: Harper & Row.

Duckworth, Eleanor. 1991. Filmed TEDx Talk. "When Teachers Listen and Learners Explain." www.youtube.com/watch?v=1sfgenKusQk.

Fariña, Carmen, and Laura Kotch. 2014. *A School Leader's Guide to Excellence: Collaborating Our Way to Better Schools.* Portsmouth, NH: Heinemann.

Fletcher, Ralph. 1996. *A Writer's Notebook: Unlocking the Writer Within You.* New York: HarperCollins Books.

Fullan, Michael. 2005. *Leadership & Sustainability: System Thinkers in Action.* Thousand Oaks, CA: Corwin.

———. 2014. *The Principal: Three Keys to Maximizing Impact.* Hoboken, NJ: Wiley.

Gladwell, Malcolm. 2008. *Outliers: The Story of Success.* New York: Back Bay Books, Little, Brown and Company.

Glover, Matt, Ellin Oliver Keene, and Ken Robinson. 2015. *The Teacher You Want to Be: Essays About Children, Learning, and Teaching.* Portsmouth, NH: Heinemann.

Goldberg, Gravity, and Jennifer Serravallo. 2007. *Conferring with Readers: Supporting Each Student's Growth and Independence.* Portsmouth, NH: Heinemann.

Graves, Donald H. 2004. *Teaching Day by Day: 180 Stories to Help You Along the Way.* Portsmouth, NH: Heinemann.

Hargreaves, Andy, and Michael Fullan. 2012. *Professional Capital: Transforming Teaching in Every School.* New York: Teachers College Press.

Harvey, Stephanie, and Harvey Daniels. 2015. *Comprehension & Collaboration: Inquiry Circles for Curiosity, Engagement, and Understanding.* Portsmouth, NH: Heinemann.

Knight, Jim. 2009. *Instructional Coaching: A Partnership Approach to Improving Instruction.* Thousand Oaks, CA: Corwin Press.

Lehman, Christopher, and Kate Roberts. 2014. *Falling in Love with Close Reading: Lessons for Analyzing Texts—and Life.* Portsmouth, NH: Heinemann.

Mraz, Kristine, and Christine Hertz. 2015. *A Mindset for Learning: Teaching the Traits of Joyful, Independent Growth.* Portsmouth, NH: Heinemann.

Numeroff, Laura. 1985. *If You Give a Mouse a Cookie.* New York: HarperCollins Books.

Paterson, Katherine. 1977. *The Bridge to Terabithia.* New York: Thomas Y. Crowell.

Paterson, Katherine. 1978. *The Great Gilly Hopkins.* New York: HarperCollins Books.

Pink, Daniel. 2009. *Drive: The Surprising Truth about What Motivates Us.* New York: Riverhead Books.

Ray, Katie Wood and Lester Laminack. 2001. *The Writing Workshop: Working through the Hard Parts, and They're All Hard Parts.* Portsmouth, NH: Heinemann.

Renwick, Matt. 2017. "Professional Reading: When Do We Find the Time?" *Reading by Example.* https://readingbyexample.com/2017/02/21 /professional-reading-when-do-we-find-the-time/.

Renwick, Matt, and Heather McKay. "Reading by Example." *Reading by Example.* Accessed June 23, 2017. http://www.readingbyexample.com/.

Rosenblatt, Louise. 1978. *The Reader, the Text, the Poem: The Transactional Theory of the Literary Work.* Carbondale, IL: Southern Illinois University Press.

Rylant, Cynthia. 1982. *When I Was Young in the Mountains.* London: Puffin Books.

Schmoker, Michael J. 2007. *Results Now: How We Can Achieve Unprecedented Improvements in Teaching and Learning.* Heatherton, Victoria, Australia: Hawker Brownlow Education.

Sergiovanni, Thomas J., and Reginald Leon Green. 2009. *The Principalship: A Reflective Practice Perspective.* Boston: Pearson.